PREFACE

My earliest memories of the Cape are of myself as a small child staying in a rented cottage in Chatham for two weeks each summer. After school let out, my family packed up suitcases, bug spray, beach blankets, pails and shovels, Coppertone #4, a blue plastic dinghy meant to tow my siblings and me across the water, and our just-bathed basset hound, Samantha. Then we joined the onslaught of traffic heading for the Cape. Our tiny cottage off Cockle Cove Road had grooved teak walls that I loved sliding my fingers down and rustic living room furniture that was remarkably comfortable to lounge in. I would sit there after playing in the pine needle-covered playground while my dad cooked on the barbecue and the fog rolled in. But what enchanted me most about the trips were the sheer beauty of the tidal creek and the grace of the houses that seemed to smile at you from the roadside on warm summer afternoons.

Shortly after I turned twenty-six, I moved to Brewster to live with my German girlfriend, who was there for the summer thanks to a cultural exchange job program. And there my love affair with the Cape was rekindled. I developed an ever greater appreciation for Cape Cod homes. My girlfriend, who had been nurtured on a continent where architectural detail was more universally admired, would remark to me at night how Brewster's houses seemed to have eyes and a life of their own. Passing by these architectural gems during late-night strolls, we always felt like we were in good company.

There were also moments that summer when we wondered if we were in the presence of ghosts. When we necked on the jetty at Breakwater Beach in pitch darkness, a howl of wind or the sound of nearby footsteps—which may have been just our imaginations—would prompt us to dash back to the parking lot. In our campground cabin, we sometimes woke up startled by twigs snapping outside and the screen door slapping—even though it was latched. In the dead of night, it was tempting to believe that ghosts were responsible, but by morning I always put this theory to rest, reasoning that there had to be a more logical explanation. In my hometown of Seekonk, Massachusetts, I'd never heard firsthand ghost stories and never really thought about the possibility that ghosts could be real.

Four years later, my friend Gary got me thinking about ghosts again. We had worked together for a year at the former Cape Cod Baseball Card Company and were now thinking of collaborating on a book about the Cape. One day he told me that he'd grown up hearing ghost stories on the Cape and thought it would be interesting to talk with the people who told these stories.

Much to my own surprise, I was enthusiastic about Gary's proposal. If nothing else, I loved the idea of getting inside the soulful Cape homes I'd long admired. I would be brought along on tours of historic structures with borning rooms and beehive ovens, minister's closets and Christian doors, Lower Cape cellars and hidden attic spaces. But what resonated with me was the passion occupants expressed for their homes and their humility and respect for the past. I felt a special kinship to these houses from having seen and experienced them through the eyes of those who know these homes intimately. I hope you will feel that way, too.

I am indebted to Gary not only for suggesting this book but for his wisdom and openness while writing it. There is no overstating how valuable those qualities were in getting to know our interviewees as people and recording their stories without condescension or embellishment. I quickly came to see these stories as Gary did—something as natural to the Cape as coastal fog and kettle ponds. Contrary to my expectations of encountering people on edge and seeing ghosts around every corner, we heard a diverse set of reactions to the idea of living with a ghost. I'd expected to find only the unusual, but I found something closer to normal. I met thoughtful, well-grounded individuals who related their experiences with humor and insight.

While I still tend to dismiss things that go bump in the night, I've found it difficult to refute the credibility of the people who participated in this book, or the concrete specificity of their stories. No matter how you interpret them, Gary and I believe you'll enjoy these stories as an introspective look at what it means, and has meant, to live on the Cape.

Dan Gordon

INTRODUCTION

"We don't have ghosts on the Cape," the ranger at the Salt Pond Visitor Center informed us with a confident smile, unaware I was a native. "Cape Codders are too practical."

Fortunately, this good-natured gentleman was one of only a handful of Cape Codders Dan and I had asked, at various institutions ranging from nursing homes to VFW posts, who hadn't heard a local ghost story or had one of their own. One thing the ranger was right about, however, was the practical nature of Cape residents. The main reason this book may seem a little different from others of its kind is that Cape Codders take their ghosts in stride, usually accepting their experiences as natural, positive, and even comforting, rather than eerie or spooky. That's not to say that all of the experiences described within were pleasant, or that you might not be unsettled by some of them. But, for the most part, the people we interviewed, including those whose first encounters made them jump, came to regard their experiences simply as a part of their lives, albeit an unusual and intriguing part.

Cape Cod may have a higher than average share of such tales, but a tradition of ghost stories can be found in most cultures. Maybe you've had an experience yourself. If not, you probably know someone who has. If you ask your family members, friends, and coworkers, chances are at least one or two of them will tell you about a ghostly experience they've had—and it may be their first time telling the story, either because nobody ever asked them or they felt uncomfortable sharing it.

During my youth, I, like most people, became curious about whether there is an afterlife or a spirit world. My curiosity was piqued mainly by the fascinating tales I occasionally heard from friends and relatives, particularly my aunt, who still lives on the Cape. She told her stories with a refreshing simplicity and directness. Because she described each instance matter-of-factly—no cobwebs, bats, or rattling chains—as if it were just another occurrence in her life, her stories were more memorable to me than if she had called special attention to them or tried to make them scary. It's this down-to-earth aspect of the Cape's storytelling tradition that we've tried to recreate in *Cape Encounters*.

Having grown up in a house where my family and I heard unexplained footsteps and bangs and crashes in unoccupied and unfurnished second-floor rooms, I would often wonder what was behind the noises; whether events like these could really have supernatural causes. Part of what appealed to me about this project was the opportunity to try to find out for myself. I naively hoped that if I talked to enough people who had these experiences, I would hear enough anecdotal evidence to enlighten me. But after listening to several dozen Cape Cod residents tell their stories, I'm still wondering.

From the time we scheduled our first interviews, I also looked forward to hearing these people describe how they felt during their encounters. Too often the books I had read on ghosts de-emphasized the human element in favor of the ghost story, and they usually didn't provide much of a sense of the qualities that made these people, and subsequently their experiences, unique and memorable. After all, it's their conclusions, philosophies, attitudes, and senses of humor and wonder that personalize these stories and allow the rest of us to relate to them.

Ghost stories are mysteries. So it shouldn't be surprising that people who claim to have had ghostly encounters might wonder how they should be explained. If the people in our book show a tendency to philosophize or ponder what might be behind their experiences, they're only displaying a natural curiosity. If we presented these stories without including these very human reactions, I think something thoughtful and profound would be lost.

Cape Encounters does not pass judgment on these stories, nor does it endorse or deny the existence of ghosts. The main purpose of the book is to describe the telling of ghost stories as an entertaining and thought-provoking aspect of life on Cape Cod.

For as long as I can recall, I've had an abiding sense of how fleeting life's moments can seem. But I find meaning and inspiration in the idea that whether or not we believe in ghosts, the past stays with us—partly in the old homes, buildings, and roads we continue to make use of, and partly in the actions and decisions taken long ago that continue to influence our lives. So meeting others who share a similar appreciation for the past has particular significance for me. Many of the people who participated in this book expressed deep respect for history and tradition. Their encounters made them more aware of their surroundings and of the lifestyles and accomplishments of the people who lived in their homes before them. They have a greater realization of the impermanence of people, places, and things, rather than taking them for granted. Conscious of their own transience, they see themselves as custodians of these historic places, maintaining them for the benefit of future generations.

We weren't able to verify every historical detail told to us. Such claims as whether a building was used as a stop on the Underground Railroad can be very difficult to prove. Old stories offered as explanations for the alleged ghost phenomena, usually by trying to identify the ghost as a real person from the past, sometimes don't hold up under close inspection. What historical detail there is in *Cape Encounters* is there as background and local color to enhance the stories and illustrate the narrator's attachment to a particular location.

I do want to mention the vital contributions made to this book by my co-author, Dan Gordon. Any praise this work may receive is mainly due to his tireless dedication, hard work, and patience. He strove constantly for quality. His enthusiasm and encouragement inspired me to turn a vague notion into a reality. Dan is not only an outstanding writer but also a great human being, and I will always be indebted to him for his generosity, guidance, and wisdom. I'm fortunate to have him as a co-author and even more, as a friend. Quite simply, I'm a better person for having known him.

Working together on this project was fun and rewarding, and it enabled us to meet a lot of engaging, helpful people. And now it's their turn to speak. If you listen carefully, you might hear some other, fainter voices, too. So while you're reading, if you happen to hear a sudden noise, take a quick glance away from the page. You may be able to catch a glimpse of something, just for an instant, out of the corner of your eye. . . .

Gary Joseph

REVERBERATIONS

*Bruce MacKenzie, a seventy-two-year-old international busi-
nessman and former professor at Boston University and United
States Military Academy at West Point, was cordial and
refined. He wore dark tan chinos and a red sweater. His sen-
tences sometimes trailed off, and he often interrupted himself to
rephrase his thought. He sat up and talked faster in response to
our questions, stimulated by conjecture and trying to rationalize why he has experienced a ghost for as long as he can remember, and explain what gap exists between science and the understanding of ghosts. Later in the conversation, he belly laughed
at his remarks, especially as he tried to typify the ghost.*

*We were seated in comfortable upholstered chairs in the
living room of his seventeenth-century full Cape in Orleans.
It was a sunlit room with a low ceiling with exposed beams.*

C ape Codders were always heavily sea oriented, making their living one way or another from the sea. Sometimes they'd go away for months and come back with boats

full of salt herring or cod. Shipping traffic developed after the Revolution, from Boston down to Virginia, especially all along this whole Cape down through Fall River, New Bedford, Providence, New Haven—"haven" meaning harbor. And the ghostly story of this house is that at Nauset Inlet and Nauset Beach there were land "pirates." Mooncussers. In the nineteenth century there were hundreds of shipwrecks out there. Schooners would get a little too close to the shoals. Of course, in those days, if you had strong storms, squalls, and fog, you could easily get lost. So the Mooncussers developed a strategy of putting lanterns on the shoals on foggy or stormy nights so that ships thought they were channels. And that would attract ships to the shoals, and then they would kill the people and take the treasure.

One of the inhabitants of this house in the 1810-1830 period was part of an Orleans gang of Mooncussers. After a number of these successful ventures, the local constabulary apparently were lying in wait for them over on Nauset Heights. Though the gang escaped, the constables pursued the owner of this house back here. He knew they had recognized him and were coming for him. So he went in the attic and hanged himself, and he has been here ever since.

We have certainly heard him, and his presence has been quite real over the years. And that goes way back into the 1920s and '30s.

My mother and father would hear voices in the attic, and we would hear strange cries very often at night. My mother designed these hooked rugs you see on the floor and taught people how to make them. When she was doing that and was very busy, apparently, he would respect it; but when she would go to bed or just started reading, he felt that it was time for socializing, in whatever limited form he could do. And my mother would say, "Oh, shut up and go to bed." I grew up with it. He was not a hostile ghost, but, apparently, he tended to just want a little bit of company from time to time.

I can remember sleeping upstairs on Thanksgiving in the mid-1930s and hearing strange cries and definitely being frightened enough to come downstairs to the bedroom where my mother and father were sleeping. And they said, "He won't hurt you." They had absolute faith that the Mooncusser was still here.

My mother died in 1970. She had lived down here alone. (I had been away a great deal of the time.) One winter my daughter Pia and her husband stayed in the house. She had heard it before, but this was the first time that the phenomenon was extraordinary. She was sitting in this room with her husband and the snow was, oh, almost a foot deep outside. And they were sitting here in the evening, after the sun had gone down. They heard voices and tapping on the door. They tried opening the door, but it was frozen. They looked out the window, and they couldn't see anything, and then she heard darker, heavier voices and also some children's voices by the front door and the door by the kitchen. So they put on their winter clothes and boots and went out, and there were absolutely no footsteps and no traces of anybody. If someone had bodily come up, they would have seen it.

Since then, I've heard it upstairs primarily. I go up to the attic to put things up there. I don't expect to find anything, but I can see. . . . You've got the old boards about that wide. But I don't think he's solely in the attic. And very often I feel a presence in the room, still. I'll feel somebody standing there. I've felt him everyplace. I can be on the bed, and I can feel something there. Every once in a while I'll go in the kitchen and I'll see the pots start moving. The doors and windows are shut, and we're not having any Richter-scale events. There is something that is disturbing the air. I grew up with it and can definitely remember sleeping upstairs in the bedroom here, with the attic up above. I remember hearing very definite noises in there. And I remember hearing voices. But that was kind of the extent of the stories, without embellishing it. Many guests who stayed here—we've lent the house to people—come away so stressed. They would turn around and swear somebody was in the room. They'd come back afterward and say, "Really, very strange." We didn't talk about it too much. We didn't want to make people nervous.

The ghost hasn't been hostile at all. I must admit that in the last three months I haven't noticed it. But I travel a great deal. I go all over the world—in China and Europe. I'm not here a lot. But when I'm here alone I do feel someone is here. I don't think that I'm that imaginative. I don't feel I would just imagine that. I mean I'm an engineer by trade, not a mystic by any means.

He chuckles modestly.

Well, I'm afraid that's all I really have to say about it. That gives you an idea. This house is now over three hundred years old, and I think any old building that has been inhabited or used for centuries has an immanent humanity, or spirituality, about it, probably however you define it. Have you ever gone to places like Chartres in France? Or, in Europe, have you been inside these old cathedrals or very old houses? We have an old house in the south of France, about two or three hundred years old that one family had lived in for two hundred years. We have a very different feel when we're in it. We never feel alone. It's not like moving into a condominium or a new track house. I'm very uneasy in new houses. I like to feel that some of the reverberations from the past are there. I mean, this is no different from explaining what we're doing right now in physical terms. I was a communications professor and like to think as a model that we have an emitter, a receiver, and alternating current channels and all that; but, ultimately, there is an energy there that we have no way of explaining, except that somehow it gets converted from the lamb I just had into—

He laughs.

—energy. That takes a pretty mystic interpretation, if you think of that.

He laughs again and blushes.

And we can think of ourselves as no more than reverberations from the past. We're vibrating. We are here, lucky enough to be. Somehow we have energies and we're expressing them—at least, for the moment. I don't feel there's an absence of expression just because one is no longer living. There's nothing to life if you don't have energy driving it. You don't have to be a mystic to think of the reality of energies and space. I mean, I certainly think, three hundred years ago, anybody talking about radio waves transmitting pictures, they certainly would have been considered a mystic.

So, I think of the idea of a ghost as an individual whose energy or identity, even though very cloudy or lost much of the time, continues in some way. You can look at it and wonder about it, or you can just ignore it. It's just a form of rotating molecules or atoms or particles spinning around.

When I grew up down here, discussions of ghosts were pretty natural. There were a lot of abandoned houses around. Oh, I remember walking through the big Captain Linnell House, which is now a kind of posh restaurant. The house was built in the 1830s. In my childhood, that was abandoned, but it was open—anybody went in. We kids would wander in and out, around it. We always felt there was someone else there. That was not a question.

This whole area was very isolated. We used to go "fishing" on Captain Ellis's horse and cart, way out on the flats where he trapped fish in the weir, then brought them back in barrels for shipping to Boston.

But it's common knowledge that my house probably had been abandoned after this man hanged himself. He definitely was chased from over in Nauset along there where they put out these lanterns along the rocks and shoals, and that's where most of the major accidents occurred.

There's the ghost of the old Namskaket Road. Most of the time he's just present, immanent. I think that most of the time he probably feels reasonably comfortable in this place. And, at this point, there's a continuity. I've been in and out of this house for almost sixty-five years, so I'm not unknowing. It's like people who have had breakfast together for thirty years—they don't necessarily have to have a conversation.

At the moment, the ghost seems to be very much at peace. Maybe it's because I still do say "hi" to him when I come in. And I don't pretend he's not there. Maybe ghosts age! Who knows?

He laughs, shaking his head.

Do they always stay the same age? He was in his midthirties when he hanged himself.

I think of it definitely as an individual. It is still a personality. I think there's anger. Definitely emotion, anger, and frustration. But there are little children, too. I hear voices from time to time. But, as I say, when my daughter was here, she heard voices inside, but these voices included darker, heavier voices outside. And no tracks. She wouldn't—and certainly her husband wouldn't—have had an inclination to invent that.

I think this has given me an awareness, even though I'm not religious or spiritual. And I think it gives me a humility because I don't really understand the phenomenon, and a curiosity about it. Quite a lot of writing and lecturing and science didn't always have an impact.

But probably, more and more often, when I come through the door I'll greet the ghost—that type of thing. Sometimes that seems to make a difference. I feel better in the house.

FOOTSTEPS

"This house has been in my husband's family since it was built. His great-great-grandfather built it. And everyone who has lived in it has changed it a little bit," said Lee Baldwin. She shuffled paperwork at her kitchen table. Lee wrote a popular nature column in the Cape Cod Chronicle *and worked as a field guide at the Cape Cod Museum of Natural History. She had a sharp distinguished face, a friendly countenance.*

Over the phone she had sounded surprised that the Harwich Historical Society had mentioned her as someone to talk to about ghosts. "I can't think of any," she'd said. "I don't know why anyone referred to this house as haunted." She was quiet for a moment, then said, "Well, maybe it was Lynne Elston, because I once told her I hear footsteps. It's silly actually. We were both acting at the time in a local theater. I remember having that conversation as we were opening an old clothes chest that had been donated to us as a prop in the theater. But it's true that from time to time I hear footsteps. I've grown so used to them. I didn't think of them when you mentioned ghosts. I actually don't believe in ghosts."

The Baldwin family living room had paneled walls and several shelves lined with worn, hardcover books. It was a very comfortable setting in which to hear Lee's perspective on her home's history, her sense of family and continuity, and her ambivalent feeling about ghosts in the house. We sat around a cozy antique table with a tapered edge.

You can put the tea right on the table. It's old and was here when we moved in. I don't like to finish furniture. We have had five kids grow up here, and we did not want to fuss with polishing. It wastes a lot of time. I can show you the picture of the people who built the house.

She gets up, removes it from the wall, and brings it over.

A lot of them were sea captains on a coastal schooner. We have a Bible that lists all the people who were born here and died here. It was in the house when we moved in. We have telescopes and the original navigational charts. One couple had eight children, but only one of the children had children. Three or four died as babies. One died at sea when he was about twenty. One, I don't know what happened.

Now, you want to know what I hear? When I'm down cellar, I'll hear what appears to sound like footsteps go across the kitchen, then disappear into the living room. Just casual—you know, ch-ch-ch-ch! Four, five, or six steps—

like someone crossing the room, and they get to wherever they were going to go.

My husband will hear steps a lot, too. And, for some reason, I've decided this is a woman because I've been in this house for thirty-something years. I've been doing the same chores that every woman who has lived here has been doing. The rooms are still the same. The bedrooms are still bedrooms. The kitchen is still where the kitchen was. So I just figure it's a woman doing housework. If it's anybody—if there's such a thing.

It happens about once per month, usually when I'm home alone. Or my husband and I hear steps if we stay in the bedroom reading, when it's quiet. It's a light step.

When I first heard the steps I can remember hollering, "Hello?" Then there'd be no answer. So, after a while, you stop hollering, "Hello."

We moved here the summer of '57. I don't think I can remember anything happening early on. It was more after we started to remodel. The house was in bad shape, practically falling down. We used to let the kids paint on the walls because we knew we were going to have to change them later. Then they wanted to do it when we put the new walls in.

They're not like that now.

She laughs.

See, they're all grown up.

I used to say, "Oh, we should have a séance, or use a Ouija board or have somebody in that picks up stuff." I read a little bit about it. But I don't know. Sometimes it's best to leave well enough alone. The house is very peace-ful. We use a lot of the furniture that people have been using for a hundred and something years. I don't mean the stuffed furniture, but the chairs, desks, and this library table.

Maybe I'm a ghost agnostic.

Because I would never say it's impossible. Otherwise I guess I wouldn't be saying I heard footsteps. I wouldn't admit it.

It's one of those mysteries. Over the years you just accept it. If a lot of other things happened, you would say, "Now I've got to really investigate this." We don't have doors slamming or anything like that here.

Sometimes I feel like I have company, but it's a com-fortable feeling. Maybe that's why I thought it was a woman. There have been a lot of women in the house who have taken care of the house. I'm the fifth.

The house has always been in the family, and I feel it should go to the children. We have never even discussed selling it. I feel like I'm a temporary tenant, and that it's going to go to the kids.

From the bookshelf, she retrieves the house's original Bible. She seems to be curious to see it again and leans over the book as Gary pages through it.

I think this Bible was here when the family moved in. Old Bibles are common in New England.

She turns to a list of entries of births, weddings, and deaths—all handwritten. She leans in closely, placing her finger on one of the names.

Those are the people who built the house. They were married, "1842, First day of May." Her maiden name was Burgess. These are the children. Some of them have got the same first name because siblings with the same name had died and the parents would reuse the name for their newborns. We used pretty much all these same names with our children.

She continues reading down the page.

This is so lovely.

Joshua C. died in sea in 1852. So many of the children died in sea. That's mainly the reason I think the Bible should stay in the house. Actually, we have bought a new one, and we're supposed to be entering everything into it. You have a sense of duty with a house like this.

VIEWS

After our interview, Jean Sour had strongly recommended that we take in the view at the end of Longnook Road in Truro. As we got out of the car in the beach parking lot, we were drawn almost instinctively to the edge of the sand cliff with a hundred-foot drop to the beach. While we'd both been to numerous breathtaking spots along the National Seashore, this was one of the few where we felt so mesmerized that we had no interest in journeying down to the water. Large waves were breaking, and the sunlight shimmered on the water. Enormous dunes rose steeply on either side of us. Mist hugged the beach to the north and south. A seal popped its head up and watched an unaware couple walking along the shore. Jean described this as a spot "full of wonders," and we agreed.

Jean's rambling, white house sat approximately a half mile up Longnook Road from this spot. The road itself traveled through one of many narrow, flat-floored valleys that traverse the outer Cape from east to west. The hollows were bored by spring water traveling along the surface of the glacially deposited sediment that comprises Cape Cod.

Jean was sensitive to the ecology of Truro and to the moods that different areas of the Cape cast on locals and tourists. She reserved special affection for the Lower Cape.

An interior designer who lived and worked in Rye, New York, she used her home seasonally. We arranged to meet on a Saturday morning. She planned to return to Rye later in the afternoon.

As we approached the side door to her house, she called out from an upstairs window. "Hi. Come on in. I'll be with you in a minute."

We passed into her kitchen. A sliding glass door offered a view of a narrow backyard. Coffee was percolating. The phone rang. Jean came into the kitchen. She was wearing a white cardigan and a gold bracelet, and she had pleasantly tousled hair.

She led us to a family room with sharp white walls and dust particles visible in sunbeams. A very large fireplace across from the window had matching brass plates above it on the wall. The room's old hardwood floorboards had large nail heads. A copy of Yankee *magazine was visible on a nearby table, next to the book* Inside the White House.

She settled on a red suede chair to the left of a white couch with soft pillows where we'd taken seats. She began talking fast, in a gravelly, elegant voice. She lit a cigarette and, as she talked, she waved it back and forth in the smoke to emphasize things she said.

T he house is from 1758. As the story goes, it was inhabited by a sea captain, one of the Rich family. He blinded himself with his own boom in Philadelphia. He had a black servant called Pomp. Pomp was the only black man on this part of Cape Cod, and he was desperately lonely. He went out and hanged himself by Pomp's rock—that's a rock in back. And he became our ghost. Maybe an unresolved life. What constitutes a ghost? I've always wanted to know. What do you have to be to be a ghost? Not all souls become ghosts.

Anyway, he's the fellow. He lived in this house in the former kitchen or keeping room. That's where he slept and that's where you usually see him. He wanders through here quite freely. He's been seen upstairs. He goes into the middle house. I've never seen him past the kitchen, although I have had a renter who has. I don't know what they're confined to. I suppose they can go anywhere, can't they? As a matter of fact, I think he wanders. I think they can travel the world, can't they? These things fascinate me.

She swings one leg over the other.

I suppose he could go to Europe if he felt like it. Or Africa. And I wonder why sometimes they don't. I think there's something about that next world or level where he dwells that is restrictive. I think there are restrictions and I just don't know what they are.

My daughter and my son certainly have seen him. It's very hard to describe what I see when I see him. You don't really see a form. You don't look at it and say, "Oh, you're a lawyer," you know, or "You're a fisherman," or "You're a black servant." It's kind of gathered haze. Sometimes it's just fleeting. It's almost like a shadow. But I've sat in that room in there and seen him go through the dining room. He's gone almost before he's seen.

And it's not in the mind's eye. No. Honest to God. In your mind's eye, you picture things, there's a projection. But that's all internal. This is strictly an external thing. It's not in my imagination. I wouldn't will him here.

I don't think he frequents this place as much as he used to. Then every now and then I feel him again. It's more feel. It's almost like a tap. It's almost like this.

She gestures with her cigarette at her own smoke.

You know, but it's denser. It's transparent. It's just a coldness, and you feel there's somebody there besides you.

I've come to live with him very peacefully. He's benign. I have gotten to feel in the last couple of years that he's almost protective. In the middle of a strange and scary night when the wind is blowing down that valley, I feel as though he's here to help me, not hurt me. In the beginning I didn't feel that. I didn't know what he was about. I was terrified.

And I'll tell you, the energy changes. I can sit in that room a lot and kind of feel that he's stumbling around. It's a different energy. Really, it's almost charged. Kind of the feeling after a good thunderstorm. You know how it cleanses and it's almost static? I mean, today it feels soft. And it's not the weather that's doing that.

Her son, R. J., comes in and reaches over her shoulder with a piece of toast with jelly. As he leaves she points to the door leading from the room we're in into a back room.

That door won't close at night. I blame everything on Pomp. I kind of do it in a funny way. If something goes wrong you say, "Oh, for God's sake, Pomp." But when I hear "bang" and things like that—when something peculiar happens again and again, I blame Pomp.

Some people are just more sensitive to that kind of presence than others. I mean, I think the majority of people who live in this world could go through this house for the rest of their lives and never see or feel or touch it.

My son, who was a realist, sat in that room one night and watched one door open and shut, and then four steps later the other door opened and shut. And it has a latch. He watched the latch go up, the door open, the door shut.

Now, my mother is an elderly, proper, logical Boston Brahmin. She's a no-nonsense lady. She's very effective; she's very strong. She's old. She's ninety-three. She'd heard about this ghost and pooh-poohed it. We came down here one night in the spring, and I noticed the next day that she didn't look as though she felt well. I asked her how she slept and she didn't say anything, but the next night she asked if she could sleep with me. "I really don't want to tell you this," she said, "but last night, I woke up in the middle of the night and felt as though somebody was pulling my covers off of me. I was wide awake on the edge of my bed about to fall, and the covers were being pulled from the bottom of the bed. I sat upright in bed and just felt this terrible cold and I got up and I was scared."

She got up and went into the bathroom and turned on the light. And she said, "I just felt I had to get hold of myself." That happened, and she's loath to admit that. So there's another experience.

A renter this summer was staying in the bedroom off the loggia. He said he went to bed and lay down and, about five minutes into trying to go to sleep, he smelled this putrid odor. He rolled over, and he thought, "Well, maybe the water has turned in the bouquet." So he got up, smelled the water, and it wasn't rotten. After he lay down again, he said it became so heavy that it was palatable. He could taste it. He said, "Hideous odor. Suddenly it dawned on me, and I turned, and I said, 'Please, leave me.' And within five minutes the air had cleared." Now, I hadn't ever met this man or told him of Pomp.

I just got this letter from him. And the heading of the paragraph where he described this event read, "And now about things that go bump in the night." He had a number of encounters with Pomp. He was from Philadelphia.

She puts her cigarette out and moves to the edge of the chair.

I am told that we had a painter working in the middle house. She looked through a peephole and saw something, and she walked off the job and never came back. I wasn't here for that.

Then there was another house, farther down the hollow, across Route 6—I think he's been seen over there. Construction workers smelled cigar smoke while they were working on it, and there was one corner where the nails wouldn't stay in. Workers would find their tools moved. They'd put them on a windowsill and find them across the room after a coffee break, things like that.

More mischief than malice. I think he was probably a very kind man. Maybe I knew him once in another life.

It makes me sound as though. . . I mean, the average person, someone reading your book, is going to think, "Oh, that woman's certifiable. She's off the wall. But, he's here! It could be we're just not going to see him today. I've had a guest come wait all weekend just to talk to him, and, of course, you think he'd appear? No. I don't know how you talk to a ghost.

So maybe you've got to get into the inner workings of each individual. The ghosts are within us. Or else why would the mind's eye be reacting that way? I mean, are we all a great conglomeration of souls that have lived before? Or are we each the same soul manifesting itself differently each time? And the ghost we see is perhaps somebody we've lived in a past life. This rolls around in your head at three in the morning if you've had an experience of this kind. And there certainly are those who believe and those who don't. I think the belief is the key. It's like God, isn't it? You believe or you don't, and there's a commitment to that. Not that you're making a conscious commitment to believe in a ghost or not, but it's something that you have room for in your mentality or you don't. There could be twelve thousand souls walking around in this room for all we know. If that's the way you go, you know?

I do think at times, being a sane, highly social person who dwells in a sophisticated world, there's not an awful lot of room for this tale I'm telling you with my average friends. They look at me and say, "Sure, Jean, have a martini, darling." Or something like that. They may question nuclear physicists on atoms and things. But that's not what I want to question. There's something going on. And I don't think the majority of the world is open to it, out of fear or lack of time.

And I don't know what you found with all your other ghost areas, but there's something magical about this little plot of land. I mean you have to live here awhile, but I've never had anybody come and stay, or even work on the place, who hasn't said there's something magical about this. There's something that draws you. It's enigmatic. It's not easily verbalized. There's something that draws you—almost a polar charge. You get down here and you can't leave. You feel almost removed. I think time moves differently in this tiny little space.

Honest to God. I believe that. It's just this little enclave; it's just this little area. There's a wonderful water system. There's an aquifer on Longnook Road that gives you some of the best water in the world. Back toward Route 6, there was an Indian camping ground. I'm referring back to the 1600s and certainly earlier. You walk down there and you can almost feel that, again, there's a presence. If you were to just come someday and wander around, in six hours you would feel a time warp. It's kind of like a place out of time.

But—I said to my son coming down this time, I haven't been here in a month. I think of this place in the abstract when I'm in New York because I become a paper person, or a fax person. A computer person. And I think of this place as if it's just one pain in the neck. The maintenance. I mean, you can see it's big, and I think I've got to get rid of it. I get in the car, and I'm in Connecticut, and I start to salivate. I can taste the Cape. I can anticipate the smells and the earth. Once I am here, I get out and the first thing I do is go into the garden, look at the flowers, cut the Easter bouquet—it's calling me back to a much simpler thing, which I think is a much more valuable thing. I'm rooted here. Maybe that's a good way to put it. You put me in the soil and I'll grow. We had Thanksgiving here last year, and it was the most glorious day of my life. This is the Thanksgiving part of the world. I mean, between Pilgrims, the corn, and the crisp clean air, this is the place to have Thanksgiving. This is an Ice Age miracle. It's what I call this end of the Cape. It is. You look at those dunes, and if that doesn't take your breath away! If you're agnostic and you look at those dunes, what are you gonna believe in? Something. You got to go to the end of this road. Don't go home without going down there. Get out of the car and just look! It's mind-blowing. The beauty of that great expanse of Atlantic. You see all kinds of things out there—seals and whales, and floes and dunes. Oh, I'll never talk to you again if you don't go there. This place is loaded with history. And maybe a couple of those guys are hanging around here, too. The Pilgrims got off a boat with scurvy and sickness and dead babies. And this was their first landfall. Pomp must have endured suffering. I would think Pomp's loneliness must have been unbelievable because, first of all, he was poor. He was entirely dependent on the kindness of others, and he was the only black man here. I think he was probably direct from Africa. And my contention is that the captain probably picked him up on a ship in the West Indies, or in the Southern part of this country, and brought him back. Or maybe Pomp wanted to get out of the South. Maybe the Captain offered him freedom. Then he got here and looked at the dunes and thought, "What do I do?"

I wander spiritually. But I certainly believe in something better than man. Because we don't do it very well. As you grow older you have to believe in something. I mean, why else is there all of the turmoil and the pain? I look at ants and roaches and things, and I think, they've got their own little colony. I wonder sometimes if there isn't an even greater civilization up there looking at us as we regard ants. Does it just keep expanding? None of us know. And ghosts don't tell you.

You could really get into it and never think of anything else. But if you work, you don't have time to do that.

She laughs.

They're early-in-the-morning thoughts. Or long walk thoughts, I think.

You don't perceive Pomp, do you? It's hard when sun is streaming in windows, isn't it? Yeah, the mood changes. It's here and then it's gone. Curious place to be.

THE GHOSTLY ENSEMBLE

After spending some time in Provincetown, one can come to feel that all of its time-honored public buildings and historic homes are loaded with ghosts. The eccentric quality of the town, its maritime location, the ramshackle layout of its structures, and its remote, bittersweet atmosphere combine to create the impression of a hamlet permeated with supernatural energy.

At the center of one area of town rumored to harbor the paranormal lies the Fairbanks Inn, where it is said a Revolutionary War soldier dressed as a minuteman haunts one of its fifteen rooms. The building dates back to 1776, as evidenced by the year painted in gold on the green wooden sign in front of 90 Bradford Street. This is when Captain Eben Snow finished building his house with wood taken from his vessel in the King's Navy.

The Colonial structure is a "Captain's House" in the Edwardian style. Commonly dubbed a "square-rigger," it's a two-story box with twelve-over-twelves four across on both levels. The building is called a "brick-ender," because its east and west walls are made of fourteen-inch thick, ivy-covered Dutch bricks brought back as ballast by Captain Snow. It is one of only three brick houses in town, Norman Mailer's and the old newspaper building being the others.

The current owners lovingly maintain the inn's traditional appearance, filling it with period antiques and saving vintage wallpaper dating back to the mid-1800s. Under the oldest layer of wallpaper one of the owners recently discovered horsehair, which was used in plaster in former days. The lobby in the rear of the inn has French sliding glass doors, white wicker chairs with padded cushions, Oriental throw rugs, red umbrellas, and chocolate chip cookies reserved for guests. Just outside is a brick patio surrounded by rosebushes, the Carriage House, a stairway to the top deck, garden art, and an old-time street lamp with a sign reading "Gardena St." hanging below it—a nice Hollywood touch.

This is the spot where the office doorbell rings mysteriously. It used to happen quite often, according to inn manager Char Priolo. When the bell rings out of the blue, there is definitely nobody there, says Char, because she can see through the kitchen window. If it were a person ringing the bell and then walking or running away, she claims, they would have to move extremely fast to avoid being seen. She says the bell works fine otherwise, and there have been no incidents lately, even though the bell mechanism hasn't been changed, which would seem to rule out a short circuit.

Char, who performs as a vocalist in a local band called The Fabulous Dyketones, which plays 1950s and '60s rock, says a ghost is often seen at the Gifford House, another

"Captain's House" on nearby Carver Street. She adds that several housemen, receptionists, and bartenders have seen a male figure sitting at a table in a basement dance club called Purgatory. The specter, who wears a captain's hat, peacoat, and red scarf, is said to strike a contemplative pose, looking downward while holding a pipe in his right hand up to his mouth, and leaning his left elbow on the table.

Char says many of Provincetown's ghosts are fishing people, giving as an example an incident that took place in a house that she used to stay in on Central Avenue. Apparently, the lady of the house was mixing cake batter when she turned to see a man dressed in a yellow rain slicker, pants that bloused out of his boots, and a blue cap. At first the woman smiled, but suddenly realizing this was a stranger, with annoyance she asked the man what he was doing in her kitchen. At that moment she blinked, and the man vanished. When she described the apparition to her mother-in-law, who lived upstairs, she was told it was the ghost of the mother-in-law's husband, who died at sea. Recognizing his picture in an album she had never seen before, the woman listened as her mother-in-law explained that she'd seen her dead husband many times, watching over her.

Char is a historian for the Unitarian Church on Commercial Street and says the church is notable for having a ghostly choir. Char was alone downstairs in the building when she claims she heard the group singing. She waited ten minutes before daring to walk upstairs to confirm the source. When she reached the top of the stairs, she found the second floor quiet and empty. A man named Oscar who was sexton at the church heard the ghostly chorus all the time, says Char. Oscar lived to be ninety-three, and his long memory included recollections of looking up and actually seeing the ensemble dressed in coats.

Tucked away behind the Fairbanks Inn is Six Webster Place, a private residence. At night the red three-quarter Cape with a porthole-shaped window and white picket fence basks in the glow from the nearby Pilgrim Monument.

Mario Lebert, a former owner of the house and current proprietor of Perry's Liquors on Tremont Street in Provincetown, discovered two small, weathered old gravestones lying under the home while he and his partner were renovating it to make it a guesthouse.

The home had been empty for twenty-four years when he bought it in 1985. After temporarily moving the gravestones to improve the building's foundation, he started hearing footsteps.

"When I was working on the house, I used to hear them upstairs. I'd go upstairs, figuring it was my partner, but he was gone. He had gone to the lumberyard."

He heard the steps intermittently for about six weeks. When he redid the foundation and put the gravestones back, they stopped. Then he opened his house as an inn, and his guests reported hearing unexplained noises. Some weeks after he bought the place, a neighbor brought him an article about the house from a 1930s edition of the *Boston Herald*. According to Mario, the article mentioned a mischievous ghost and "different noises and crying from beyond."

"I really didn't give any thought to the noises," Mario says. "I know that they didn't scare me. In fact, I don't think I'm a believer."

FAMILY SPIRIT

Very often a ghost encounter will enhance a family's enjoyment of an older Cape Cod house. The subtle encounters
Adelaide Edgar had in the Brooks House in Harwich
absolutely delighted her children and instilled a deeper appreciation of the history of their 1750 full Cape with its secret
hiding spots and a massive white chimney with a black stripe.

We visited Adelaide in her latest historic abode – a
small, Wedgwood blue home, tucked away down a dirt road
off of Route 28 in Harwich. Pine trees provided shade in her
driveway. As we knocked on her screen door, we admired a
boldly colored abstract painting hanging from her front
patio. She called us in and came over to greet us. She looked
youthful and energetic, and we were surprised to learn later
that she is in her seventies. She guided us into her living
room, her dog following us, nuzzling us. Along the way,
she showed us her art studio, a light and airy room filled
with her work, including portraits, a painting of a former
building at the Chatham Fish Pier, and landscapes from

*Sanibel Island in Florida. One of the most striking paint-
ings was an almost mystical rendering of the firing of an
orange grove when a frost comes.*

I began restoring antique houses in 1971, and I restored
two houses in Florida on Sanibel Island, where I lived.
Then I came up here with my large family, and we lived in
the Brooks House in the summers. The first thing we found
that was unusual was a whole area under the attic staircase
that was most likely a hiding spot for escaped slaves as
part of the Underground Railroad. My children had been
running up the attic stairs, and the top two stairs were
loose. When we jiggled them, they came out, and we found
this secret area. The children were in and out of that place
like jack-in-the-boxes. We found notebooks, coins, and a
shoe in there.

There was an enormous fireplace in the house—I mean,
you could walk into it. There also was a beautiful beehive
oven. My children and I were all just fascinated with this.
The dining room had beautiful beams and what had been
the exposed floor of a loft above the dining room, and it
was very impressive. The keeping room had huge, beautiful windows that went from the floor all the way up to the
ceiling. It was so exciting being in that house that one
wonders how we ever could have observed a presence.

Now, I restored houses. I did not renovate. I didn't
change windows and insulate walls. I restored homes to
their original condition and saved the glass and learned
how to do a lot of things. I was also very interested in
removing wallpaper samples. I took specimens of the wallpaper and tried to preserve them.

One day I was on my hands and knees in one closet, upstairs under an eave in a rather long room that had been used as a nursery, pulling hand-made linen off the back of this closet wall. The linen had plaster underneath it, so I was intent on what I was doing. I had a stack of old paper around me. And all of a sudden this perfume fragrance just overwhelmed me. It was a foreign fragrance and very pleasant. The room was just full of it. I thought, "Who has come upstairs to say hi?" Because people dropped in all the time. I got up and went out of the closet. I turned around and no one was there. I called and walked out of that room and down the hall. The fragrance was in the hall at that point, and it was strong. I went on down the stairs following the fragrance and checked in the keeping room. Halfway into the room, I stopped smelling fragrance. At that point, I went out to the side of the house where the driveway is to look to see if someone was just pulling out, and there was no one out there. This same experience of smelling perfume happened on another day in the front room. I was rather surprised and mystified by it. I had spoken to the children, especially the girls, because Monique was living in a back room. And Monique said no, she'd never had it happen.

There was no way that fragrance had come from outside. There was something that was in the house, and it was very spooky. After I sold the house, I was quite friendly with the man who bought it. I would stop in occasionally and see the men who were renovating the house and talk with them. The owner was there one afternoon, and I spoke with him about it. I said, "Have you found any ghosts?"

He said, "No, not really. But it's the funniest thing. There must have been someone with a lot of perfume in this house at one time. We have come across it a couple of times." He and his wife were sleeping in what was used as the front bedroom, which had originally been used as a justice-of-the-peace courtroom. And they were awakened one morning at four o'clock. The room was just full of the same wonderful fragrance that they had smelled when they were restoring the house, and he said this happened a lot.

I said, "You know, I have had that happen too when I was upstairs."

The Brooks family had owned the house until the 1920s. Sara Brooks was the last one to live in the house, and she died there. Upon her death, all the papers that she and her sister had accumulated were given to the Harwich Historical Society, which is now housed in the Brooks Museum. Because I lived in the house and I was the third owner, I became very interested in the Brooks family. I read about how Obed Brooks had married a French woman, Clementine Guigon, who eventually died at quite an early age, leaving everyone terribly grief-stricken. Reading the letters that Obed wrote and reading the notations in his diary, I learned that Clementine was a rather glamorous feature to have come from France into this small town and married into this family and had a bunch of children. It was my deduction that it was she who was still hanging around. I think probably that was her fragrance that had come through the house. I have traveled—not a great deal but enough to know it was a very exotic fragrance. It wouldn't have been Sara, because she was an old maid. Going back through the rest of the Brooks family, none of the women in the family would have had some type of fragrance like that in their possession. Henry Cobb Brooks eventually had an office at Lewis Wharf in Boston. But until then the Brookses weren't that well off. The women in the family would get up at four in the morning and go over to Herring Run and catch enough herring and come back to be at the Brooks House in time to get breakfast for the men before they went out to wherever they were going.

Another unusual thing in the house was the cigar smoke. Late in the afternoon, very often when I walked across the keeping room, I could smell it right at the bottom of the stairs. It would last ten or fifteen minutes. There was definitely a puffy cigar smoke somewhere in the air and, halfway up the stairs, you said, "There it is again." But then you kept on going upstairs, and then went back to the kitchen, doing whatever you were doing, and then it was gone. There was no missing it. Not at all. It wasn't a musty smell from the dark. It was bone chilling! Because no one I knew smoked cigars, and with a house full of seven children and no other adults, if anyone smoked anything, it was cigarettes. But no pipes and no cigars.

At first, I was the only one who smelled it, but after the first two or three times, the boys came up to me and said, "Hey, I gotcha! I smell it too!" This went on for all five summers.

The children were very interested. They wanted to know about spirits and ghosts. Maybe we stirred something up. I mean, it was just a zoo. There was very seldom a breakfast, lunch, or dinner that we didn't have ten or fifteen people. Every summer we drove up here we had a Volkswagen van with a nanny and her child, and four or five bicycles in the back of the van, and a couple of cats in a cage, and two or three dogs, and the rest of the children. It was very fun. The children were very interested in the history of the house. As a matter of fact, I think the second year we were in the house, my daughter Jane wrote a history of the home. Not for school—she just came out with it. I think the spirits stimulated the idea of history.

The first experience I had of smelling the perfume was really very chilling. It was very odd. But as it happened more and more, it made me become more open to the idea that it has to be something. It brought me up short and opened me up to whole new possibilities as far as life is concerned. That there's more there than I'd been flirting around with. It made my life larger. I suddenly began to think about all of this knowledge that people have today. Maybe some of it was prompted by whatever was floating around. I mean, I'm together. I'm practical. I know how to do patchwork with plaster. I know how to put a wooden roof on a house. I know how to hang doors. I can't do it, because I'm not strong enough to do it now. But I'm together. You're not talking to someone who is really off the wall.

She laughs.

But I'm of an age where I am open to a lot of things now that I was not open to at one time.

In retrospect, I had a similar experience in a very tiny old house on the West Side of New York City, just before you got to the docks. It was a beautiful little house. We had this feeling about it, and it would have been perfect for us; but it didn't work out at the time. That was the first experience of walking into a structure that people had lived in for a long time and having a feeling about it. We filled the Brooks House with children, and we brought someone out of the woodwork, and they were sort of sitting back and watching.

H. K.'S LEGACY

Charles Terrell works for the Agricultural Department in Washington, D.C. In the summer he and his wife, Sandra, run Academy Place Bed & Breakfast at the intersection of Main Street and Route 28 in Orleans. One late spring evening in their upstairs bedroom they awoke to a door slam, which they attribute to the ghost of H. K. Cummings.

We settled on a couch in the dining area, facing a long antique dinner table and the entrance to the kitchen. Charles sat relaxed in a soft chair to our left. He proceeded to give us a lengthy history of the house and the characters who had lived in it. Sandra occasionally stepped out of the kitchen to add something or playfully tease her husband that he was off the topic.

He spoke genially and deliberately, barely restraining his joy. He was short in stature and endearing, upbeat and humorous, obviously fascinated as he speculated about what may have transpired among the house's former occupants.

M y first experience with Cape Cod was tenting at Nickerson State Park in Brewster, which would have been about 1950. The tents were all World War II surplus, and they sat on a wooden platform. I can remember the ice man coming by every two or three days, chipping away at a block of ice with a pick, and dumping it in a metal box where we kept perishables. That was our introduction to Cape Cod.

My parents decided they wanted to open a guesthouse. My father was fleet superintendent at a bakery. He scraped together enough money, and my parents bought this house. They signed the papers in this room, on their anniversary. Present was Miss Elizabeth Brown, who had inherited this home from a Mr. Henry Knowles Cummings, who was pretty much "Mr. Orleans." Mr. Cummings was the man about town. He owned the downtown area. Most people just called him H. K. He was the photographer who took pictures of Lower Cape shipwrecks.

H. K. bought this house in 1887 and the following year married Theresa, the woman who lived across the street here in the great big white house on the hill. Her father was a sea captain. H. K.'s father was a sea captain. H. K.'s grandfather was Captain Linnell. So there were a lot of sea captains in the family. And there was a lot of money. I have to admit that even in the time that we moved here, people would say, "If they were so well off that they owned the downtown area, why would Henry live in such a fairly simple, unelaborate home?" And it's a good question. I think part of the answer lay in the fact that H. K. had not only a wife, but a mistress: Phoebe Brown, Elizabeth Brown's mother. In his will, he left this house to Elizabeth. He left his summer home, which is two miles from here on the salt water river that comes in from Pleasant Bay, to Phoebe. He also left cash, which amounted to about eighty percent of his estate, to Phoebe.

Let me divert for a second. I'm the national environmental coordinator for the Water Conservation Service in Washington, D.C., and across the Mall is the National Archives. There I discovered in the 1910 and the 1920 censuses that Phoebe Brown is listed with her husband, whose name is David. So we have a scenario.

He springs up, comes over to the coffee table, and opens an album meant for his guests as an education of the history of the house and shows us first a picture he calls "Welsh Rarebit Party" taken in the same dining room under a kerosene lamp. On the left side of the photo he identifies H. K., his mistress, her grandmother, and others engaged in upbeat conversation. Then he covers that side of the photo. Theresa and several dour-looking women are sitting on the right side of the photo. "Theresa and what I call her support group know what's going on. And obviously, they did not approve of it at all."

Next, he shows us a photograph of Theresa behind the wheel of a sailboat in the town cove. "She has such a powerful, determined look on her face, like, 'Boy, I can sail this vessel as well as a man.'"

He returns to his seat.

So, why do I go through this to tell you about H. K. Cummings? He really leads us to why you came here today. I don't think that either Sandra or I ever thought that the house was haunted. That had never, ever occurred to us. And I'm not sure if "haunted" is the right word to use.

My father had passed away in 1976, and my mother lived

here alone after that. Her room was this little room here off the dining room. My brother and I determined in 1987 that she couldn't live here alone. So the plan was that we would move her to Tampa, Florida. She would be about ten minutes away from our sister; and she had her own nice little home in a community of older folks. And about that time my brother said to me that Mother told him there had been a series of occasions when she awoke in the middle of the night to see a nice young man who was all dressed in white at the end of her bed. My brother said he sat at the end of the bed, and when I talked to my sister, the way it had been relayed to her was that he stood at the end of the bed. My mother told both of them on different occasions. During one of my brother's conversations with her, he asked, "Well, do you feel unsafe about this whole situation?" And she said, "No. Most of the time I just roll over and go back to sleep."

And my mother was a high-strung person. I can remember as a boy when she had a nightmare, as she was apt to do when she'd sleep in the wrong position, she would absolutely yell at the top of her lungs. It was just blood-curdling.

When my sister asked her on several occasions, "Are you sure you were awake?" she said, "Yes, I'm totally awake." My brother asked her one time, "Well, do you talk to him?" And she said, "Yes. Then I go back to sleep." I mean, talk about weird.

I never heard these stories directly from my mother. I think probably she didn't want to worry me since I was the youngest. So I never heard about this until my brother told me. And when he did, we both just laughed. We thought it was the funniest thing in the world—and really never thought much about it beyond that. There was no reason to. She felt safe here. And I think that's why we could take it lightly.

At any rate, the second incident occurred after my mother moved out. Sandy and I decided to open a bed and breakfast. So, from January through June, I took one week off each month and we slaved cleaning this place up. It would not be unusual to get up at six in the morning and work until one or two in the morning the following day, then spend four hours sleeping, then start again; you have to understand that really nothing had been done to the house since my father died.

We took everything out of the house and stored it in the garage and in the cottage that's out back. So there was literally nothing in the house. In March of 1989, sometime in the middle of the night, both Sandra and I were awakened from a sound sleep by a door slam. I mean, it was not just closed—it was slammed.

And I sat bolt upright in bed and said, "H. K., you get out of here! This is no longer your house." Then I realized what I had said and felt so embarrassed.

I said to Sandra, "You have to talk firmly to ghosts." I mean, what else can you say? This is not a normal conversation that you have at two in the morning.

But the strange thing about it is neither of us was afraid. A door had literally been violently slammed in the middle of the night, enough to wake both of us up from a sound sleep. And yet, in spite of that, we weren't afraid. If we had felt fear, what would we have done? We would have gotten up and we would have investigated.

I knew what it was. And both of us just rolled over, and it just left our mind. We went right back to sleep.

In the morning, none of the doors was positioned any differently than when we had gone to bed at night. Nothing was open that had been shut. Nothing was shut that had been open. The doors were as we had remembered leaving them when we went to bed at night.

And it wasn't as though a limb fell off of a tree and fell on the roof or something. I mean, it could be explained in some other way. Anything could be explained in many different ways. But there was no other rational explanation. It was as if I took the door right beside you and just slammed it shut. Even if you were napping you would know that was a door that just slammed.

But let me tell you something else that's an emotional response of mine. Even though I spent many summers here growing up, when I came back in 1989, the house didn't feel right to me. It didn't feel like it was the house I had left, the house I knew. And it wasn't just because it was empty. It was strange. Yet from that point on, after I had told H. K. that this wasn't his house, I felt it was our house.

I mean, you could make an emotional leap here and say that was H. K. leaving. And he slammed the door behind him.

Now these are emotional reactions, and irrational, if you will, but then it was very real. And, by the way, all my training is in science and technology and that's where I make my living and that's what I depend upon doing and doing right. But this isn't one of those things you explain via science or technology.

I guess my conclusion is that if there is a spirit that abides in this house, it is a friendly spirit that means no harm and maybe even has left. Who can say?

It was just one of those things that happen—a part of your life. It's just there, and it doesn't adversely affect me.

If you think about it from a rational standpoint, what could a spirit or a ghost do? I think a burglar can do more harm than a spirit. Most of the time we live afraid of those things we haven't met.

So, I don't have any real trouble believing that these things happen. I mean, I personally do believe that something visited my mother on several occasions over the years, and that it happened just in the way she said, and that she was not dreaming. Although she very possibly could have been dreaming, I honestly believe that she was not.

I do a little bit of teaching in my work. In fact, I have a course coming up on an ecological approach to determining water quality. And I try to teach my students, "Don't look for the magical answer that will make everything fit into a nice little box." Especially when you're dealing with nature; it doesn't work that way. Nature is an entire spectrum. Those intergrades between our answers are the ones that baffle us the most. Sometimes there are no answers, and you have to make that leap from the science and technology, leaving the matter unresolved in your mind or simply leaving it as an open question.

I would say this allows you to look into areas that you previously would have thought were closed to investigation, simply because you can't explain them scientifically. Once you've reached that point, it's amazing how many things you can start to look at clearly. In fact, the course I'm teaching is about a book that a professor from the University of Tennessee and I wrote called *Water Quality Indicators*

Guide. I won't get into a long story, but it's basically an eco-logical approach to determining the quality of water. It is not a water chemistry type approach, and traditionally we do water quality determinations from water chemistry. But both that professor from Tennessee and I had to make that quantum leap away from looking at the test tube—the color of the water, the color of the test, so many milligrams of this, so many micrograms of that—and say that maybe you don't have to do that to make a water quality determination.

It's sort of the same thing here. Maybe as a younger man I wouldn't have had the capability of looking beyond the traditional answers about spirits and ghosts or what-ever you want to call them. But at this point in my life it's a perfectly plausible jump, and I don't have any trouble with it. I just accept it better.

So, that's the story of this house and some of the people who have lived in it. By today's standards, I think they lived rather extraordinary lives. They didn't appear to be constrained by all the social rules that we have. When the topic of H. K. came up one time, one of the old-timers in town said to my parents something that has stuck with me. He said, "H. K. was a psalm singer on Sunday and a hell-raiser on Monday."

You know, we always like to remember the best things about people anyway. So, while there are some negatives on behalf of H. K., he was always doing something for the town. He donated land. The very first thing in his will is one thou-sand dollars that he gives to the church. He organized the first phone company in town. He was interested in seeing the town grow. But he also had a side that emotionally had to be very devastating to Theresa. It had to be. I mean, how do you explain to someone, "Well, my mistress is coming back today for the summer." How could you ever tell that to your wife? Or maybe he didn't but his wife knew it.

And yet here was a man who, when the four-mast schooner *Calvin B. Orcutt* was stranded between Orleans and Chatham in a storm on December 23, 1896, walked for three hours in the snow up to his waist. The people of Chatham could see the ship and tried to get a message to Orleans, where the life-saving station was, because the ship was on the Orleans side of the inlet. The telephone line wasn't working. So, a Mr. Nickerson from Chatham traveled through snow to the telegraph station. A telegraph was sent to the Orleans Depot. The telegrapher, Amelia Snow, tried to get someone to carry the message to the life-saving station, which is in Tonset, a mile or two away. The first man—he was from the livery stable—said he wouldn't send a horse out in that weather for anything. The second man, a young man, said he'd only do it for five dollars. That was a week's wage. Finally, H. K. heard about the plight and offered to take the message. And H. K. walked from probably about eight o'clock to eleven o'clock at night to reach Tonset. I mean, how do you explain H. K. in those terms?

Is he a very good person, or is he a very bad person?

To conclude that story, they didn't get to the ship until about one o'clock in the morning, ten hours after the ship was stranded. They weren't able to rescue anyone. The ship was a total loss. But nevertheless, you have to look at what H. K. did.

I SCREAM, YOU SCREAM

T he first house Jan Potter ever built owes its existence to a ferocious winter storm. Sharyn Lindsay, Jan's wife at the time, said the project started as an idea to use the rough, tar-covered ship's pilings that the storm washed up along the National Seashore. Digging the foundation was the next step. At the work site on Newcomb Hill in Wellfleet, Jan had excavated about four feet of sand when, to his surprise, he uncovered an ancient fire pit ringed with oyster shells. At the time, Jan thought it was an interesting discovery but not significant enough to inhibit work on what became, in Sharyn's words, a "marvelous structure," a modern, hand-built, post-and-beam house with a freestanding, hexagonal sub-building connected to the main house by a deck. The sub-building had two stories; the second was an extra bedroom, while the first floor served as Jan's artist studio.

For the first three or four years, life was normal in the

house, although Sharyn could sense an unknown presence in the sub-building. Whatever it was seemed innocuous at first, until one night when Sharyn and Jan were sleeping in the hexagonal section, which was not their usual practice. Sharyn suddenly awoke screaming at the top of her lungs. Her usually mellow cat, which routinely slept on Jan's chest, stood at the end of the bed with her back hunched and tail up, howling and making horrendous, other-worldly noises that aren't usually heard from a cat. The crying, bawling animal tore downstairs, so frightened that she deposited piles of excrement on the steps.

Sharyn believes her pet may have been reacting to her thoughts moments before waking. She'd had the sensation that a third person was in the room and felt impending harm. "Someone is here," she agonized. "Why can't I see them?" When she finally stopped screaming, she looked over at her husband, who she says was moaning. Sharyn claimed this continued for an inordinately long time before he eventually awoke.

Sharyn, who described herself as a "tough cookie," never slept in the room again. And after dark she wouldn't even enter that bedroom.

Some months later, a good friend of the family on Jan's side came to stay in the guest bedroom. During her first night there she sat up in bed screaming, terrified. Later she described an experience identical to Sharyn's, about which she had known nothing. Shaken, she left later that day. Some months later, Jan and Sharyn sold the house. They never told the new owner about the screaming incident. They eventually became friends, and the new owner told

Jan that guests who stayed there woke up screaming. Jan recalls the woman telling him of five or six similar instances.

Although Jan never had the experience himself, he still ponders the incidents in the bedroom: "With all the old houses in Wellfleet, why did it have to happen in a new house that I built?" Sharyn says Wellfleetians are usually tight-lipped unless talking to a good friend, so one can only wonder if others who have stayed in the second-floor guest bedroom wake up screaming.

INTRUDERS BEWARE

Dorothy Baisly talked haltingly in a soft voice that belied she was an inquisitive, free-spirited senior at Chatham High School. Seated in her stone-terraced backyard at a glass table with a yellow tablecloth that fluttered every now and then, she spoke with fondness of her grandmother, Clair Baisly, a noted author on Cape Cod architecture and the former chair of the Chatham Historical Society. The family dog, Rowan, a mixed breed of Border collie and German shepherd, lay affectionately at her bare feet. Dorothy had adopted her from the local shelter.

My grandmother was a historian, and she knew a great deal about Chatham and gave me a great interest in the houses around here. She died when I was eleven, so I don't remember a whole lot of her stories, but she was into just about everything having to do with Cape Cod architecture and history. She would give tours of the town showing all the houses that were reported to be haunted. I always liked haunted houses. When I was about thirteen, my grandmother came back once. I sat up in bed, and I looked over in the corner and I saw not really a person, but the outline of someone. I knew it was my grandmother. I sat there for a couple of minutes and then I said, "Oh, cool. She's gone now. That's it." I think she was just checking on me. It was kind of nice.

There's a house right on Oyster River that a lot of my friends had said was "haunted," if you want to use that word. I was with a couple of friends one night after a party. We were pretty bored, so we decided to go down there and check it out. It's only the second house around here I had ever tried getting into. You get bored around here, you know.

She laughs.

We found a bulkhead door to the basement that was open. We went inside, and upstairs we found this log sitting on the dining room table. So we read it. It basically gave a brief description of the house's history. The person writing it said they liked to call it the "cathouse," because it was owned in the 1850s by this man who lived in the city and would come down on weekends and entertain his mistress.

After reading the log, we went through the house. Sheets were covering the couches, and all the beds were made up beautifully. It was a really, really nice house. It had five or six bedrooms. I didn't find anything that seemed peculiar. But we were standing in the den, which is basically all windows, and we heard a bang in the kitchen. We thought, "Whatever. Wind, right?" All of a sudden, we heard people talking in the attic. It was two or three voices chattering away. But we'd just come down from the attic, and there was nobody in the attic. So our reaction was, "Yeah, we're leaving now!" I ran down to the basement, went up the bulkhead, and jumped into my friend's car and sat there and waited for everybody else to come out! A couple of my other friends said they were in the house one night, in the same glassed-in den, and they heard someone walking in the attic. They thought maybe it was the house settling. All of a sudden, a big spotlight was shining in their faces. They guessed it was from a source outside. They said, "Let's get out of here. The cops are here!" So they fell to the floor and crawled out of the house, and there were no cops outside.

A lot of my friends had been in there and seen and heard nothing. They'd go in there and sit around, chill, and just check out the house.

There's a house that's been renovated on Cross Street, which runs off Main Street downtown between the town hall and the church. It has been moved back away from the street, and the foundation has been redone. But it's a very old house. And it was up for sale a few years ago. My best friend and her mother were planning to move, and they were looking at that house. They were standing on the sidewalk and looked up and saw this person walking across the windows on the second story. But they're in different rooms. Somebody kept walking in front of the windows like he was going through walls. So my friend and her mother said, "No, we're not buying that house!" And they just left. There's definitely something to it; you can look at the house and sort of get a sense of a presence.

There's another very old house farther down on Cross Street. The lady who used to live there died in the house. A bunch of my friends and I decided to check out this house one day because we noticed that nobody had been in it for years. We went all around the house, and there was no way of getting in because all of the doors and windows were nailed shut from the inside. I don't know how somebody managed that and got out because there's no basement. Unless they went up to the second story and jumped. The house was actually falling apart. The upper part of the front wall was falling off. One of my friends put his hands through a broken window trying to push up the storm window, which was slightly open, but he couldn't. He didn't cut himself, which was actually lucky. But as his hands went through the window, he said he felt this cold breeze go over his whole entire body. He shouted, "I'm outta here!" And he ran off.

We did a lot of background checking on the house. There was an old electric bill in the mailbox addressed to a Mrs. Alexander. We went to the library to see who owned the house, then later went to check the town records. The librarian had said, "Oh, yeah, I remember a Mrs. Alexander. She was an old lady. She was losing her memory. And her husband had died about ten years before she did." The librarian used to work at the public market, and Mrs. Alexander would go down and buy dinner for herself every day. But she'd buy dinner for two people. She'd be talking about her husband coming home quite often. But her husband had been dead for several years.

So we went back to the house after the research to try again, and I walked up to the back door. A friend of mine decided that he found a way in. And all of a sudden, I kind of felt something and said, "No, I don't want to go in." All I could feel was evil coming out of that house. A bunch of my friends wanted to go in the house on another day, and I discouraged them. I thought Mrs. Alexander was still in there waiting for her husband to come home or something like that. I didn't want her to be any more ticked off than she already was.

THE BIG HINT

A bike was lying on its side in the dirt driveway of Bob Wiles Jr.'s blue full Cape. A Dunkin' Donuts mug sat on unfinished wooden stairs. Bob opened the front door. "Come on in, guys, move fast." A well-groomed West Highland white terrier was at the door wagging its tail. "Sophie, you gotta stay in." Bob's wife, Carol, leaned momentarily into the living room and greeted us. We took seats on a couch, and Bob sat perpendicular to us on a mini-sofa. Many handcrafted angels hung on the wall above his head. Rubbing the top of his crew cut, he said, "So like I said, there's not much to my story." His nine-year-old son walked into the room, ready to sit and listen. Bob said to him, "You didn't wash up or nothing. Wash up, brush your teeth, take care of business, please."

I lived in a house on School Street, here in Wellfleet, for approximately five months in the winter of 1974. During the course of the winter, the lady who owned the house, Georgia, started renovating upstairs. Prior to this, no one was really aware of anything particularly strange going on in the house. But it became evident after she started that there were a number of things that were definitely a little on the bizarre side.

I'm not sure, at this point, in what order things happened, but I know that one recurring thing was even though the burner technician had been there and serviced the boiler a number of times, it kept having this backfire problem. It would blow the exhaust pipe off the furnace and soot the house up. I know that happened at least three times. The burner serviceman couldn't believe that it was still happening. There was no reason for it because he had cleaned the burner. There was plenty of draw on the exhaust pipe. It's not in an unprotected area, so wind wasn't causing it, or anything like that.

Bob's son enters the room and quietly takes a seat next to his father on the mini-sofa.

At the time, living there were the lady who owned the house, her boyfriend, her youngest son, his girlfriend, my girlfriend, and myself. Several times during the course of the winter, we'd be sitting around the living room. And while old houses creak and groan, there's a difference between normal house noises, such as wood settling, and what sounded very much to us like somebody walking around upstairs. It was very distinctive. We were used to the house and knew if somebody were upstairs, there were several places that you could walk and step that made very distinctive, separate squeaks, groans, and so forth. You could envision someone walking across one room, across the hallway into the next room, and into the attic portion.

A few of us had done a moderate amount of painting and so forth upstairs. When we remounted the latches on the doors, we re-positioned all of them so they would function, and you could shut the door and it would latch and it wouldn't accidentally just swing open. Whoever got home first would find either the doors all open when they had been shut, or all shut when they had been open.

You know how normally you lay your things out on the bureau, like jewelry boxes, odds and ends out of your pockets, or whatever? That whole winter there was never any time that I left anything on that bureau and didn't find it moved when I came back home. At one point, it was the source of a rather severe argument with my girlfriend because I had accused her of doing this deliberately to sort of play with my mind. But then a couple of times when we were both out of the house, things got moved around. It wasn't just on top of the bureau. It was little things, but all over the room. Dave, Georgia's youngest son, accused us a couple of times of messing around in his room. Once everyone accused my girlfriend of going through all their stuff. She was so upset, she moved out. Nothing changed. Then Dave accused me of rifling through his possessions and so forth. And I just said, "Hey, back off. I haven't been here all day." So, over the course of that winter, I think it became apparent to everyone who was living in the house that there certainly was something there that to a certain extent was a little malicious. Mischievous. Not really deliberately malicious.

We never actually saw anything move with the exception of a couple of doors in the house that had the annoying habit of just opening when we were sleeping—you'd hear the attic door just swing open. It was really evident because you'd feel a draft and it would just swing open, and you'd find yourself waking up and looking at this open door and expecting to see somebody there. There wasn't anybody there, of course. A lot of it I could explain away if we hadn't done the work with the latches and hadn't been doing any of the painting there. But I can't really explain it. It seemed to me that whatever was going on in the house could be because someone was very upset at the renovations going on upstairs. When we had the problems with the boiler, that stopped our renovations for at least a couple of weeks. We had to just plain clean the house, repaint the ceilings that had just been blackened to the point where you couldn't leave them like that.

Georgia had a couple of Irish wolf hounds that she used to keep in the house. The dogs, we decided, were playing with our minds, because, in unison, they would turn and just look at the set of stairs, which was very unnerving when you were sitting there—sometimes, by yourself, just reading a book—and you saw them all of a sudden perk up and just look. I understand that animals sometimes do that—they maybe catch a shadow out of the corner of their eye that they decide needs their attention. Trude, the younger hound, on a couple of occasions, did an about-face. The hair across the top of her back stood on end; but even though this dog was couch-sized she was kind of a scaredy-cat anyway, so it didn't take much to spook her. The wind whistling under the door was just as liable to scare her as anything. The dogs never really liked to go upstairs, but I think that was more because the stairs were very steep for their frame. When you came in the front door, there was a very steep set of stairs going to two bedrooms upstairs. That's the classic Cape. There are a million of them around here. Those dogs were about 150 pounds, and even as big as this guy is here—

He nods to his son, who had remained seated by his father, absorbing his story.

—he could throw a saddle on one of them and ride him.

His son laughs, and asks in quiet wonder, "What happened to the dogs?"

I don't know. I don't know if she still has them. But there's certainly a presence in the house, in my mind. Why it's in the house, or what the history is, I don't know. The main part of the house originally came from Billingsgate— you know, this island off Wellfleet that sunk into the ocean. So, the initial part of its history may be untraceable.

My girlfriend claimed she saw something. But I'm not sure that she was sober, because I know that was right after Christmas and everybody in the house had been partying all day. She could have been seeing pink elephants. But, maybe not. She said she saw a young man, but I pressed her for more details. She picked an inappropriate moment to talk about it, and the rest of the people in the house just jumped on her. They figured she was telling stories, and they didn't want to hear it. As soon as their reaction was apparent, she just shut up about it. She wouldn't talk with me about it. I don't know whether she was afraid I was going to react the same way.

These events created a lot of dissension. They were probably the number one reason I moved out of the house, along with a rather unsatisfactory relationship with my girlfriend. It was time for me to leave that household because it was just too crazy there. Even under the very best of circumstances, it still wouldn't have been an ideal living situation.

If you reported things moving around in your room while you were out, it just made things seem incredibly worse. It's hard to describe. I care even now very much for all of these people. Back then I felt very much in a caring situation, but it seemed like these people were—how do I explain this? It seemed like they were being influenced to a certain extent. Maybe just by everything that was going on in the house. They weren't really making their best choices in what they were saying and doing. I had known all these people for a while, and it seemed like everybody had a short fuse. Situations that should have been handled very mildly became very volatile.

At one point, I went with my aunt to Florida to help her move out of her house. After I left, Georgia's boyfriend and her oldest son decided they were going to redo my room while I was gone. Instead of patching the plaster, they ripped it all out. I came home to find they hadn't covered any furniture, any of my clothes, any of my belongings. Everything was covered with broken plaster. At that point, I thought, "Well, okay. That's the big hint, I guess." It was time to go.

After I moved out, Georgia's oldest son's relationship with his girlfriend, which seemed fairly stable until that point, went down the tubes. Her youngest son's relationship also went down the tubes. The guy who Georgia had been living with for two years left. This was all within a one-month period. And my relationship was already sort of canceled. So, you know, I can't really point blame at any one thing, but it's clear to me that there was an influence there.

I went back once to visit Georgia because I was going through a bunch of stuff that I had and found something that was hers. So I brought it over to her. At that point, all she wanted was to get rid of that house. She did sell it within a year or two.

I occasionally see those people because some of them still live in town. But there isn't that closeness that there was then. It's kind of like, "Oh, hi, how 'ya doing?" "Fine. How are you?" We were not death-till-we-part friends before the falling-out, but we were certainly very close. I think originally any of us could have gone to any of the others and said anything, without having any anxiety about being judged, but as I said, that got winter-weary. And I really don't think it was a matter of just plain cabin fever setting in, because all of us certainly had more than enough outside interests not to be stagnated into any kind of too tight relationship where it was overcrowded. Most of the time, there would be three or four people at home, and it was really no big deal.

I was going through a lot of changes then. In 1974 I was like twenty-two years old. Looking back, I can say that was part of a great big growing-up process that I was going through. My wife asked me this morning, "How come you never told me about this?" I'm like, "There are a lot of things that I haven't told you about, only because they've ceased to be important to dwell on." In a lot of ways that was a very good part of my life. In a lot of ways, it was a very painful part of my life. At this point, it's ancient history.

GOOD NIGHT, GHOST

The guest book at the Penny House Inn is brimming with entries expressing gratitude for a relaxing, comfortable stay at this historical getaway in Eastham. But on a handful of occasions, guests have popped the question: "Are there ghosts in the inn?" Margaret Keith, the friendly, outgoing innkeeper with a cheerful Australian accent said, "One young woman wrote that she saw an apparition in her room. She later described him to me, and I was delighted to hear he was exactly the same gentleman that my daughter and I have seen."

One of the first things we noticed when we pulled into the inn's gravel driveway was how peaceful the surroundings were, even though a tall English hedge was all that secluded the property from Route 6. The bow-roofed full Cape with burgundy trim and attached buildings at right angles to one another beckoned us inside, and the interior of the inn did not disappoint. Massive ceiling beams and orig-

inal wide-planked flooring reminded us that we'd stepped into one of the older homes on Cape Cod. After a full day experiencing the raw beauty of Coast Guard Beach or walking Eastham's many fine nature trails, guests at the inn could take in a relaxing massage from the inn's trained masseuse, work out with a private yoga instructor, retire with a luxury bathrobe to their guestroom fireplace, and take a dip in the room's Whirlpool tub. How could a ghost resist kicking back at the Penny House?

Margaret gave a relaxed tour of the inn in her sandals and along the way paused many times to talk about the history of the inn. Her last stop was the dining room where apparitions have most often been sighted.

This part of the inn was a sea captain's house built in 1690. They don't know who built it, but the gentleman across the street is a Horton, and his great-great-grandmother was born in this house. At one point, the house used to be Nauset Marsh Nursery. The boards that sheathed the house extend all the way from the base to the peak. The ribs of a boat are bowed, so they used those for this roof, which explains the bow roof. It's really old. I know one ghost is Isaiah Horton III, because one of the relatives gave me an old photograph of Isaiah, and I recognized him. I've seen him a few times in the dining room and sitting room. My daughter has seen him a few times in the dining room and upstairs. The lady presence seems to stay just in the addition. I don't know who she is.

They're never menacing. You see someone in the corner of your eye. You look straight at him and see someone standing there. It's a very hazy glimpse, and it's not defined. If you turn around and look again, there's nothing. It's not scary. The first time, I thought, "Oh my, it's your overactive imagination." But he still appears every once in a while and kind of just stands there. Every once in a while the digital clock on the mantel would go crazy. It would say seven o'clock but only light up some of the lights. I don't know if it was the ghost fooling around with the clock or something electrical. A couple of times, it coincided with people seeing him or me seeing him.

Before I retire at night, I say, "Good night, ghost."

I don't see him then, but I have a feeling he's here. This is where he felt most at home. The other week, there were no cars and everybody was out. And I swore I heard somebody walking up and down at the other end of the house. It's just one of those things. He's around.

BEDTIME STORIES

The Lancy Mansion once housed a historical museum run by the Research Club, an organization of women who were descendants of passengers on the *Mayflower*. But the Second Empire-style structure on Commercial Street in Provincetown is better known today as the home of Front Street Restaurant, which offers the fine dining atmosphere of a European bistro. While there are no known ghosts in this charming eatery with antique booths and highly lacquered wooden tables, the building's upstairs apartments have inspired sleepless nights.

The cube-shaped, twenty-room mansion was built in the late 1880s by Benjamin Lancy, a wealthy merchant and ship owner, at the request of his mother, Nabby Lancy. The story told by the family is that Nabby dreamed of owning an extravagant home built of Boston brownstone, with a widow's walk where she could watch the comings and goings of her son's fishing and lumber schooners. Because of the steep cost of bringing brownstone to Provincetown, her son instead built the home with wood cut to resemble stone blocks. The siding was then coated with brown paint mixed with brownstone sand to give the illusion of brownstone.

Known to this day for his eccentric behavior, Benjamin would often skinny-dip in the harbor and walk back across the street to the house sans clothing. Another one of his pastimes was to collect horse manure from the street and use it for home fuel. When Nabby passed away in February of 1896, the ground was said to be too frozen to dig a grave. According to a letter written by her great-great granddaughter, Nabby was laid out in her upstairs bedroom with the windows kept open. Benjamin and his sister Maria "visited her every day, combed her hair, and even cut her nails when they thought it necessary. Days passed into weeks. When spring came, the body was still in its upstairs front bedroom, still being visited by doting family and friends until the neighbors complained. Family tradition relates that due to public pressure they finally buried their beloved mother, three months after her death."

The current façade bears little resemblance to the dramatic original home, except for the bracketed cornices under the eaves, the fretted dormers, and the distinctive central cupola topped with wrought iron. But that never stopped many of the building's occupants from feeling inspired by the building's past. In the summer of 1996, the upstairs tenants headed to the town historical society to learn more about the Lancy family. Inspired by an article about the mansion in the *Provincetown Banner*, they wondered if the mysterious events that happen from time to time in the upper floors are the work of Nabby or Benjamin.

Jeannine Dougherty and Charles McPherson shared the top floor apartment, which is above the mansard roofline and has a staircase leading up to the widow's walk. They often witnessed lights turning on and off seemingly of their own volition. On one occasion a hair dryer, which was put away in the closet, turned on by itself. One afternoon when Charles was alone in the apartment he saw in the bathroom mirror somebody walking by behind him.

Late one February evening, Jeannine was alone in her bedroom drifting off to sleep when she heard a door slam and heard very slow and deliberate steps downstairs. It startled her because Front Street Restaurant was closed for the off-season and the two apartments below her were empty and shut for the winter. Anyone who had a key to the house was off-Cape. She then heard the distinctive sound of the metal door to her apartment opening. Prior to going to bed, she'd locked the door and bolted it. "I literally froze in terror as I heard the footsteps come straight up my stairs toward my bedroom door and then stop," said Jeannine. "I was too afraid to leave my room, but I can assure you I had every light on in the room that night and didn't sleep."

Thomas Kennedy, who lived next door, left work early one afternoon with a fever and headed straight home. His windowless apartment was pitch-black even in the daytime. As he was about to fall asleep, he felt the bed tremble. At first he thought he was shivering from his fever. He sat up and then tried to lie still for one minute, but the bed continued to shake. "After it stopped, I was like, 'What is this?'" said Thomas. "I checked around later and there wasn't an earthquake." For several evenings after that, Thomas would wake up to find the bed momentarily shaking. But the first experience had lasted several minutes. "I was a little nervous that first time, because I thought maybe it was because I was sick. On the other occasions, I just found it a little unsettling."

A few months later, Thomas was sitting on his bed talking to his roommate when something appeared to step onto the bed then step off, as if it were the first step of a staircase. "I said, 'Whoa!'" he laughed. "We weren't as shocked as we probably should have been. By that point, I'd heard a lot of stories from even before we all moved in there, and a lot of unusual things had happened while we were there."

In the 1990s, Jeannine and Charles owned a jewelry store on Commercial Street, and most of their summer help who lived at the Lancy Mansion frequently reported hearing someone walking up the main staircase of the mansion when no one else was there. Charles was quick to point out that whatever presence is in the house is benevolent, and he feels it is just harmlessly crossing over from another dimension. "Nothing bad has ever happened to us," added Thomas. "The history of the house is already very imaginative. Having these things happen just makes it more interesting. It's like, 'Welcome to my haunted house!'"

FEAT OF CLAY

*The Cape is well known for its beautiful beaches, spectacu-
lar dunes and other scenic coastal vistas, but among its
lesser known treasures are the many quiet, winding roads
that travel through the rural, hilly terrain of the peninsula's
wooded interior. Queen Anne Road, lined in places by
gnarled trees and pines, runs from Harwich to Chatham,
meandering past former farm houses, kettle ponds, conservation areas, and eighteenth century cemeteries for victims
of smallpox.*

*Pam Black, a local potter and longtime community
activist, spent four months living in a two-story, white
clapboard Cape on Queen Anne Road that had once served
as a stagecoach stop for travelers to Chatham. She shared
with us her most vivid memories of her home.*

I moved into the house of a friend of mine. I needed a
place to stay because I was in the process of moving the
pottery studio from Chatham to where I currently live in

Harwich. It was definitely a haunted house. One thing, in particular, that happened could never be explained away. No one could figure it out. The room I slept in wasn't very big. On the other side of each one of its four walls was either another room, a hallway, or the outside. So you couldn't have run around the outside of the room and made these noises. Knocking would start about three feet up the wall and would go around and around the room. It would speed up. Da-da-da-da-da-da-da-da-da. And it would go on and on. It used to drive me nuts.

It happened quite often, and I would mention it to people and they would say "nah, nah." I believe in energy and spirits and stuff. I've tried to expand my consciousness through meditation, which may be why I'm receptive to these encounters. I don't really like to use the word "ghost" that much. But I knew that it couldn't have been a mouse running around or anything like that because it wasn't that kind of noise.

My child didn't like to go upstairs in that house by herself. When you were going upstairs, you would hear footsteps right behind you on the stairs. You'd look around, and there'd be nobody there. It terrified her. She was only three years old, and had never thought like that before.

It happened to the man who owned the place, too. Before then, he had owned a haunted house in Weymouth, and in that house he had had visions of some guy who had been murdered in the house. They went back through the records and found that someone had been murdered there.

Years ago I lived in a house on Martha's Vineyard, and a couple of times glasses floated out of the cabinet and onto the table. My brother stayed there for a while. He would be in bed, and the door would open. He'd hear footsteps. The bottom of the bed would sink. It used to really freak him out. We could never keep the front door locked—ever. It was always unlocked. We would lock it and it would be unlocked. It was unbelievable.

But the footsteps on Queen Anne Road were freaky. You'd run up the stairs, and you'd be hearing running up the stairs. It wasn't an echo. It wasn't that kind of thing. I had met the previous owners, too, and they said, "Oh, yes, the house is haunted."

FOOD FOR THOUGHT

The Bookstore & Restaurant, a family-owned-and-operated fixture on Wellfleet's Kendrick Avenue since 1964, is the setting of the first story told by Tonya Felix, a waitress at the restaurant and an actress at Orleans Academy Playhouse. The restaurant, which is famous for its locally harvested, succulent oysters and littlenecks, faces Mayo Beach and overlooks the harbor and Great Island. A wooden railing runs along the upper deck. A rusty anchor lies on the lawn near the sign for the Bomb Shelter Pub, the late-night tavern located beneath the restaurant. Oceans of Books by the Sea, the little, eclectic bookstore that gives the restaurant its name sits unassumingly behind the building.

Tonya, a young woman with blond hair pulled back and expressive eyes, was working her first summer in the restaurant when she had the following experience:

I was upstairs one day setting up the bar, and, out of the corner of my eye, I saw a big man with light blue pants sitting in a chair. I felt like he was looking at me. The only reason I even caught him out of the corner of my eye is because I thought someone was looking at me. I thought, 'How did he get up here?' I did a double take, and he was gone. It all happened over a two-second period. About two hours later, the same thing happened again. It was a regular chair, and he was there sitting off to the side—basically, checking out what I was doing up there.

So I said something to a couple of people and they reacted with "Whoa, Tonya's seeing ghosts," and all these dumb things, and I kind of laughed it off. But I told the owner, "I think I saw something upstairs." She said, "Oh, you did? What did it look like?" And I described him to her, and she said, "Oh, my God, that's my dead husband!" She said that was his height and build, and he used to wear his white shirt when he was working in the kitchen really hard. He died of a heart attack. It happened here, right outside the kitchen.

I only saw it that one day twice. It wasn't threatening or spooky, or anything like that. It was as if I were standing here talking, and I saw someone out of the corner of my eye and I turned around to look, and the person was gone. That quick.

Tonya also describes a couple of incidents that took place in her former home further down Kendrick Avenue.

An elderly couple used to live in the house. The wife used to lock herself in the closet to get away from her abusive husband. They both eventually died in the house.

My husband was in that closet, getting something down, and he felt a cold rush of air go through him. He caught his breath, turned around and looked, and saw a woman breeze through the bedroom really quickly. He felt that was the guy's wife. He didn't say what she looked like. He said, "I thought I just saw this woman."

Then I had a similar experience maybe a couple of months later. I was in the bathroom, off the same bedroom, drying my hair. I turned and saw a woman sitting on the bed. She had short dark hair and some kind of housedress, and was just sitting there watching me. I turned the hair dryer off and she kind of just melted out.

Tonya feels that she and her mother have an extremely strong connection when it comes to having these kinds of experiences.

My mother was in bed asleep in her home in Harwich. And she woke up, and there were two men who looked like they were ablaze. Later on that morning, there was a girl standing there. All of her hair had been chopped off. She was just standing there looking at her. So my mother did some research, and found out there was a church on her property that had burned down. The preacher at that church—this was back in the 1800s—was accused of murdering a girl, after accusing her of witchcraft and cutting off all of her hair.

This is just something that has been happening ever since I can remember. My mother is more into this than I am. Her theory is that because we're so closely linked, the girl could have come to either her or me.

FLOATING FLUTIST

While many a rumored ghost can dazzle the eye or raise the hair on the back of the neck, one of the more popular specters at the Inn at Duck Creeke in Wellfleet can hum a few bars and play the flute to boot. Amplifiers mysteriously turn off mid-performance when folksinger Maureen Burke performs onstage at the Duck Creeke Tavern. During duets with her brother, an unidentified third voice has often joined in. Band members from Sylvan Zephyr have seen the ghost walking onto the stage.

One late summer evening, versatile pianist Tom Fitzgerald kept jerking his head back during his performance. When the inn owners, Bob Morrill and Judy Pihl, asked Tom why he was doing that, he said, "She kept pulling my hair." During another performance, the pianist went from lead to an accompanying mode—playing four bars, stopping, and playing four more. When he finished, Bob once again asked Tom for an explanation. The pianist said, "Didn't you hear the flute?"

The Inn at Duck Creeke is a potpourri of historic buildings overlooking an ever-changing salt marsh and tidal creek. Each of the inn's twenty-five rooms has old-fashioned Cape Cod charm—some with slanting hardwood floors and wrought iron door latches from the 1800s, others with lacy curtains and antique spool beds from the Federal period; Room 34 has an exposed chimney quirkily bending through it. All guestrooms are without television or telephone. Chimneys nobly flank opposite ends of the Captain's House, which was built on a knoll on the five-acre wooded property in 1810. In addition to its eighteen guestrooms, the former sea captain's homestead holds the main lobby, the Morning Room, and two peaceful screened porches.

The Duck Creeke Tavern and Sweet Seasons Restaurant & Café rest in a building affectionately dubbed the "Hodgepodge," because it was built mainly from bits and pieces of buildings brought in from elsewhere. The piecemeal construction contributes to the building's whimsical layout. The help at the inn must travel down a set of stairs from the tavern in order to climb another set of stairs leading up to the restaurant. The oldest existing tavern in town, it is a favorite gathering spot for tourists and locals alike, and patrons often comment on how comfortable the atmosphere is and say they can feel the history. Musicians often comment that they love the acoustics. Many old-timers who have come into the bar share, "Yeah, I was there on the night that the piano player died," or "I was here on the night that that guy hanged himself on the old locust tree out there," or "I was here the night the singer died." Bob said, "At least three people have died in that building or on the grounds. Maybe that contributes to the spirits being trapped."

In the 1930s, Joseph and Eulalia Price converted the home to a guesthouse and brought onto the property whole buildings and whole sections of buildings from nine antique structures, including the Humane Huts built along the seashore to shelter wash-ashores from shipwrecks, the Wellfleet firehouse and town jail, a wharf used by the East India Company as a warehouse for tea and tin, and an Old Wellfleet Salt Works used to store fish before the invention of refrigeration. Old-timers in town will sometimes tell Judy and Bob that they were at the inn "the night Joe lost his mind." He chased Eulalia around with a machete. Staff and guests have seen this in visions. Eulalia eventually had Joe committed and took over all the property.

Judy and Bob first grew acquainted with the inn's ghosts when they leased Sweet Seasons for four years before purchasing the inn. Every night before they left, they'd latch all the doors, and in the morning the doors would be open— particularly in the Blue Room, which is one of the dining areas. Wondering if the local kids were using the building as a social hideout, they would return to the building just before dark, only to find that the doors were already open. Next, they put flour on the staircases to see if they could identify the culprits' shoes. Still the doors would open with no footprints. There was also a heavy scent of flowers in the building, like one might smell when walking into a funeral parlor.

"Since then different people have seen the spirits," said Bob. "We see them. The help sees them. On occasion the spirits have spoken to the guests."

One afternoon as Judy passed through the kitchen doorway into the lobby of Sweet Seasons, she saw a three-dimensional form, hazy like dense cigar smoke, walking across the room. "I didn't see her legs moving," said Judy, "but I could see the form go from one side of the lobby to the other. It was the figure of a woman. She was diminutive and wore a bustle. I watched her until she went right into the next room."

A young British woman, Helen Scholfield, who has been the inn's night clerk for the last six years, has seen the same woman in the lobby and also in the restaurant kitchen. Helen is most prone to see her when she's alone in the kitchen doing mundane tasks. When she's chopping on the board and relaxed in her routine, the woman dressed in white makes her appearance.

"When you're looking down, you're more likely to catch it," she explained. "The moment you look up and your other senses are engaged, your sixth sense drops. That's why you rarely see a ghost directly."

Helen attended a family gathering in England during the 2001 off-season and warmly greeted an uncle who is a medium. He hadn't spoken to or heard news about her in many years. He embraced her and said, "Helen, I see you in the kitchen. There's a woman in white standing behind you watching you. I think it's far away. Have you been to America lately?"

Several years ago, Judy and Bob gave a troubled local teenager a job in the kitchen. She would come into work, and she would feel a light tug and a little squeeze on her forearm almost every day she was there. She knew it was a woman. It made her feel very comfortable in the kitchen.

In the late fall of 2001, just after the restaurant had closed for the season, Bob had gone into the kitchen to get something when one of the gallon-sized measuring cups on top of a five-foot tall rack crossed his path and flew twenty-five feet across the kitchen. He backed up and walked out. Upstairs, he told Judy, "I do not go down there after dark in the winter anymore."

"They're everywhere," said Bob. "We don't really know who they are. But we certainly expect one of them is Eulalia. She was a really strong manager. It was her place. She would actually count the peas on the plates. Like one of the spirits that we see, she had very long braided hair and would wear petticoats, ruffles, and lots of makeup even through the 1960s."

"You want to be very careful what you tell guests," said Judy, "because you don't want to lose their business. But sometimes they'll come down and say, 'Do you have ghosts here?' You feel them out first, before you start with the stories. Because some people are terrified and they'll leave. Other people just love it, and they just want it to happen to them."

A young travel representative for a major airline hurriedly checked out of her room at the Captain's House on the second day of her scheduled five-day stay. She came back in the afternoon of the following day, looking extremely agitated, and said, "This has never happened to me before." She had gone to sleep in her room and awoke around midnight to see a woman looking right at her from a chair by the window facing the side lawn. The figure came over and put her hand over her and said, "Sleep well." The travel representative went right to sleep and woke up feeling beautiful and refreshed, then grew alarmed as she recalled the night's events.

Later that season, Judy and Bob received a phone call from a fireman who'd just stayed in that very same room for one week with his wife and five-year-old daughter. The little girl had seen a woman the whole time she was there. She kept talking about the woman by the window. She told her parents that the woman kept talking to her and reminding her to take her pills, although the girl wasn't on medication.

Staff and guests also report visitations by a pair of little girls. At a PTA event, one Wellfleetian shared with Judy and Bob that she intentionally hadn't been to the inn or restaurant since she rented Room 18 during the off-season ten years earlier. She said that she had been sound asleep in her dark room when two little girls opened the door to her room, came in, giggled, watched her, and said, "She's sleeping! She's sleeping!" She bolted up from her nap, couldn't see them, and ran down to the front desk and said, "These two little girls came looking for me." And the clerks at the desk said, "No one has come in this building all day." Judy feels that the two girls could be the daughters of the captain who built the house. One of the daughters died of influenza at a young age.

Bob recalls that one woman staying at the inn woke up and saw a staircase coming down to her bed and feet coming down the staircase. She wasn't frightened, but amazed. When she told Bob the story, he wasn't surprised because at one time a staircase had actually run through that very room.

The ghosts rumored to be in the tavern have more of a flair for the dramatic. In a tiny storage room in a far corner of the tavern, staff sometimes smell a full roasted turkey dinner with all the trimmings. The scent comes from the corner of the building that is farthest from the restaurant kitchen. In the summer of 1996, Judy and a half dozen others heard a little chamber ensemble in one corner of the basement. They went downstairs in a group and saw nothing there except storage.

One rainy, dreary night in late October, a traveler from Ireland, the innkeepers, and their friends Karen, Ed, and Pat experienced the show of their lifetimes. There was not much business at the tavern, so Judy and Bob closed up early. Then they sat down to have a few drinks at the bar with their guests. The hardwood floors, beam supports, a fireplace mantel fashioned from old railroad ties, and the Chart Bar made from a collection of period doors and marine charts spoke volumes of the past generations who had shared camaraderie in this room. On this particular evening, the innkeepers and their bar mates decided to hold a séance. Here's Bob's account:

We had always kicked around these ghost stories. And we're not very sophisticated and do not know that much about the whole thing. Someone said, "Oh, let's have a séance."

I said, "Oh, sure, that would be fine." I had had a few beers, you know. So we sat around a table, and we turned off the lights and lit one candle. We really didn't know what we were doing. We were just making it up.

Someone said, "If you'd like to come forward, please do." We closed our eyes. Our friend Eugene from a very small town in Ireland was sensitive about this sort of thing and preferred to sit to the side and watch. He saw lots of things we didn't. At one point I peeked. All the women at

the table were weeping for no known reason. There was no
reason to be sad. I looked over at Judy, who was sitting next
to me, and she was literally starting to come out of her
chair. Her chair was tilting back, and she was coming up.

"At first, I felt cold and felt like I was being pushed down,"
explained Judy. "Later I felt as if someone was literally
pulling me back, and I said 'Stop!' because it felt very physical." Ed peeked at the same time and said he would have
stopped the séance if Judy hadn't, because Karen was starting to tremble and be pulled back.

Afterward, Eugene told them that at the moment Judy
was rising out of her chair, there was a woman in the room
behind her. Karen peeked and saw a number of figures
coming from the older part of the house and moving
toward the group. "One other thing that was strange,"
noted Bob, "was that when it was all over we had lost three
hours. We thought it was ten o'clock, but it was one o'clock
in the morning. We didn't know where the time had gone."

Judy and Bob are quick to assure their guests that all of
their ghost encounters are more subtle than frightening.
They lived in the Salt Works Cottage, the oldest building
on the grounds, for eleven years and never had anything
frightening happen to them. For the whole duration, Judy
would hear light footsteps on the floor above her. It always
sounded like the reassuring footsteps of a woman walking.
"They've grown comfortable with us by now," said Judy,
"as we are with them."

FETCH

The High Toss Pizza & Cafe in Wellfleet is in many ways a typical local hangout where townsfolk congregate on quiet winter evenings to relax, have a few beers, swap stories, trade gossip, and otherwise pass the time during the slow off-season.

But the crowd at the bar discusses ghosts as casually as anyone else would talk about the weather, an oil change, or their kid's soccer practice. Jade Huber, a gregarious woman who recently celebrated her first anniversary as the owner of High Toss, recalled the moment she realized the restaurant might have ghosts. Prior to owning the restaurant, Jade operated a coffee shop in the same building. The very first day of work at the shop, she was alone prepping in the kitchen, and every few minutes she'd hear somebody saying her name from the bar area. She would search the empty building and return to the kitchen. She kept hearing her name and kept searching. "When the restaurant owner finally came in, I went, 'The weirdest thing happened.' She said, 'Yeah, the woman kept saying your name all day, didn't she?' I think the owner anticipated that would happen. I think there was a reason that she scheduled me to be there."

Waitress and bartender Sadie Biathrow, a vivacious strawberry-blond woman with inquisitive eyes, said, "We've had a lot of instances where waitresses have thought they've heard their names, and they turn around and no one's there." She herself has heard noises in the empty kitchen that sound like people mixing batter in bowls. She vividly recalled an incident where she thought she heard the sound of glasses shattering upstairs. When she ran to check, she found the glasses intact on their shelves.

Sadie has done extensive research on the history of the building. She said it's uncertain when the building was brought over from Billingsgate, a now-submerged island that was located just south of Wellfleet's Jeremy Point, but she estimates it was around 1750. For the next hundred years it was a residence, and for a few years a barbershop occupied the space where the kitchen is today. The eateries that occupied the structure over the years include Four-Leaf Continental Cuisine, Antonio's, Painter's, and perhaps the most famous, The Wellfleet Oyster House. Sadie remembers a pair of former owners who lived upstairs stating they awoke in their bedroom to see figures standing around them.

The history is there for all to see in the building's wide floorboards, old-fashioned cut nails, frosted windows, and four low door frames that no longer have doors. Outside, the historic charm of the building is accented by the pea-stone driveway, candle-marked parking spaces, red painted

wooden door with a sunburst pattern windowpane, and lit-
tle lanterns that droop like rain-drenched flowers. Jade
rented an apartment in the home across the street before she
lived above the High Toss. Jade believes the buildings share
parts of the same building brought over from Billingsgate.
She also wonders if the buildings share more than bricks
and floorboards. "These buildings have something going
on." She suspects the ghosts call back and forth by phone.
When she arrived upstairs at night, after a busy day at the
restaurant, she would go through her Caller ID, and there
would be fifteen calls from the other building when she
knew no one was there during the day.

As if that wasn't intriguing enough, the toilet in her
apartment would flush ten or fifteen times a night, her tele-
vision set would go on and off by itself, and clothes would
be mysteriously removed from her dryer and folded.
"Ghosts in old buildings are just totally fascinated with
technology," she said, "and all the things that weren't there
in the earlier days of the home." Jade feels that the ghosts in
her current apartment are a little more social. One incident
in particular stands out in her mind:

I live with two Australian cattle dogs and a golden
retriever. We were renovating last year, so I didn't have
any ceiling in the restaurant. It was sub-floors, beams, and
strapping. And you could hear everything my dogs did
upstairs. We were downstairs, sitting at the bar one night.
And we heard a thud, from the other side of my apartment.
You could hear the little bounces; the dogs would run over
and run back, there'd be a pause, and there'd be another
thud. I was thinking, "Oh, my God, I know what that thud

is. It's playing ball with my dogs. It's throwing a tennis ball." I turned off the radio and made everybody get really quiet. I mean, you can't miss a tennis ball bouncing on a wood floor. For fifteen minutes you could hear the ball bouncing and the sound of running to get it and bringing it back over, like they were waiting for somebody to throw the ball again. I said, "I've got to go check this out." I went upstairs and walked in, and they all ran to the door. One of my dogs, Abita, had the ball in her mouth. And I asked her to drop it. I assumed that after fifteen minutes, it had to be nice and slimy, and that's the only way I could know for sure they'd been playing. Abita dropped the ball. I picked it up, and it was disgusting.

I love my ghosts. We get along so splendidly. It has always been a comfort. Not a scary thing. It's like when you're a kid and you have one of those invisible friends that nobody else can see. It's totally fun.

FAITHFUL ANNA

Shirley Blakeley's home in Wellfleet is warm, cozy, and inviting. Shirley said it was originally constructed near Blackfish Creek as a general store and ship's chandlery in 1823. Passengers bought tickets there for the train that ran between Provincetown and Boston in those days. Local legend has it that the store clerk used the money collected for tickets to line his own pocket and shot himself, inside the building, when he saw a man coming to collect the monies that belonged to the railroad. Shirley wonders if the clerk might be the ghost in her home, although she says there are stronger candidates.

Shirley's home was rolled up to its present spot on Lecount Hollow Road by horse and team around 1932 by Lancaster Clark, who affectionately nicknamed his home "Stow Away." A diminutive grandmother with twinkling eyes, Shirley sat in her tiny kitchen beneath a high ceiling slanting down to a Cape Cod Christian door (paneled with a cross). The kitchen walls are adorned with framed samplers and a small painting done by Paul Suggs, a local artist and friend. The painting depicts her home in streaming sunlight with an idyllic garden and an ivy-covered tree in the fore-ground. All seven of her children have prints of it. Shirley said that in the summer, the house is almost invisible from the road, and one gets the feeling she prefers it that way. Like so many other people we'd interviewed, she showed great affection for her home's history and its previous occupants—including one who may have never really left.

There's no doubt in my mind there's a ghost here, even though I've never seen it. I have an eerie feeling about it, and I'm not superstitious. If it is Anna O'Hara, it would-n't bother me that she was settling in this house.

I bought the house in the mid-1950s from a Peter Clark, after his father, Lancaster, died. Lancaster Clark was a wonderful man, I have been told. He especially loved Halloween. He would have this whole house set up with all kinds of goodies and give the kids ice cream and drinks. He died in this house, but I don't think he is the ghost. I suspect it's his housekeeper, Anna. From what people told me about what the ghost looks like, I have a strong feeling that she may be the one. Either she or Isaac Paine, the builder of the house. Because men were very small in those days. The ghost is small. It's a small figure. Someone with a lot of white hair and sort of a round build. The descrip-tion could suit Anna very, very well.

Anna had a very strong personality. She lived with Mr. and Mrs. Clark, and after Mrs. Clark died, she stayed on in the house with Mr. Clark. Mr. Clark built her the little house across the street. Anna had already moved across the street when I bought the house. She was very, very, very possessive about this house. She would call me and tell me that my boys were climbing "Mr. Clark's tree," in my yard. And I had to remind her that this wasn't Mr. Clark's house anymore.

Mr. Clark even set up an intercom system between the two houses, which Anna made frequent use of until the speaker was ripped out of the Blakeley kitchen wall by Shirley's second husband, a man with whom Anna did not get along.

Shirley didn't feel any animosity towards Anna, because she realized she was just being protective of the property. It's this protectiveness, Shirley believes, that may be responsible for Anna's continued presence in Shirley's home. Since the ghost appears only to those who visit the house for extended periods, like a weekend or more, Shirley feels it's entirely possible that "Anna wants to know who's in Mr. Clark's house."

In 1987, my uncle, who came to live with me for the last six months or so of his life, was using my bedroom. He was a no-nonsense type of guy. He came down for breakfast one morning, and he said, "You know you've got a goddamned ghost in this house?"

I said, "I'm really not shocked to hear it, because I've heard stories about the ghost in this house."

He said, "I woke up, and this figure was at the foot of my bed." He described a short person with a lot of white hair. He told the ghost to leave and closed his eyes. But when he opened them a few minutes later, the ghost was still there. He said to it, "Get the hell out of here!" Then he shut his eyes again, and when he reopened them it was gone.

Another time, I was sitting in the kitchen with my daughter Elizabeth, who was probably then about eighteen years old, and her friend Cynthia, who was also living in the house. Then, all of a sudden, the water in the bathroom was running full force. I went in to turn it off, and I saw all the cushions from the couch on the floor.

Five years ago, my niece from New York was here with her friend. And they were in the upstairs bedroom. I didn't know my niece very well, so I know she never heard about the ghost. She came down in the morning, and said, "There was a ghost in my room last night."

I said, "Well, what did the ghost look like?"

She said, "It was a short person with a lot of hair." And she added, "It was standing by the bed. I was very frightened, but I didn't say anything. I shut my eyes. When I opened my eyes up again, it was gone."

About a month ago, Mick, my son-in-law from Dublin, had a guest from Ireland. It was a Sunday night, and he called me to ask if he could bring someone to dinner. I cook dinner for my family every Sunday night, and I told him he was welcome and I would set another place. Before he left the Cape the next day, the gentleman told Mick he had a very odd experience while he was here. During dinner something was under the table hitting and bothering his legs. He sneaked a look under the table, but there was nothing there. It was a very strange sensation and made him very uncomfortable. He said that it finally stopped but that he felt too foolish about it to mention it while it was happening. I have no explanation for it.

Just the other night I went out to dinner with another

niece and her twelve-year-old son, Trenton. They came to visit me from Florida but were not staying at the house. It was still early when we got back from dinner, so we decided we would play cards. We sat at the kitchen table and were playing when Trenton jumped up and said, "Something just hit my legs!"

His alarmed mother got up and said, "I don't know what it was, but it hit mine, too."

I couldn't explain it. We all looked under the table, and I did find a ballpoint pen on the floor in the middle under the table, but I knew that if it had fallen off the table, it could not hit two people and arrive there, some distance from where we were sitting. I asked if it could have been a mosquito or something, and they both said, "No way!"

We settled down again but when the card playing was over, Trenton asked his mother, "What could have slapped my legs, Mom?" She said, "I have no idea, but it hit mine too. I guess we will never know."

My response to this was wonder and silence. Then I suddenly remembered the episode with Mick's friend and said to myself, "This is getting ridiculous! Can it be related? Is Anna still trying to get rid of strangers?"

TALK OF THE TOWN

Just as intriguing as Barbara Vaughn's ghostly accounts of the former Brewster Town Hall are her suspicions that fate landed her in Brewster. At age eleven, she found two children's books authored by Joseph Lincoln in the attic of her family home in New Hampshire. The stories described an unnamed seaside community that appealed to her, and she asked her mother where it was. Her mother waved her hand dismissively and said, "Grandma once lived there and described it as nothing but sand and sticks." After reading the books some more and falling further in love with the setting, Barbara pledged to her mother, "This is where I'm gonna live!"

Twenty years later Barbara moved to the Cape after concluding that her recent onset of blurry vision and headaches were symptoms of a fatal disease. Her father had suffered from the condition and died of unknown cause. Barbara quit her construction job in Needham, Massachusetts, and bought a home in scenic Brewster "to enjoy myself a little bit before I died." After finally seeing a doctor and learning that she had

*migraines that were not life threatening, she went on to have
a notable career in public service. Her tenure in the Brewster
Town Hall was punctuated by suspected encounters with the
ghost of former selectman Percy Newcomb.*

*Eventually, Barbara stopped into a local bookstore and
spotted Joseph Lincoln's books, which she hadn't seen in
decades. She told the woman at the register, "I used to read
those when I was a kid!" The woman said, "Did you know his
house is in Brewster?" Barbara suddenly realized that Lincoln
may have drawn inspiration from Brewster and said, "I
wound up living in the exact same place where I had told my
mother I was going to live when I was in the fourth grade!"*

*In 1992 Barbara learned that her roots in Brewster were
even deeper than she thought when she created a family tree
for her mother. She discovered that she was a tenth-genera-
tion descendant of William Elder Brewster, who came over
on the* Mayflower *and was spiritual leader of the Pilgrims.
The town of Brewster had been named in his honor.*

In July of 1976, the selectmen hired me to work part-time
for the building inspector, Rodney Willis, and part-time
for the town clerk/treasurer/collector, Ruth Eddy. From
that time until I was elected to Ruth's position in April 1977
(after she announced her retirement), there were times
when I would have reason to go into the town hall on
weekends or early mornings before it opened for business.
I recall being aware of a strange happening on only one
occasion during that period.

In the late summer of 1976, I had to go to a job site for an
early-morning inspection. I finished the visit too late to go

home before my regular work hours, so I went in early to the town hall, figuring I'd catch up on paperwork. I used the side door and climbed up the back stairs to the building inspector's office. When I turned at the first landing to walk up the last few steps, I heard a door close right in front of me but saw nothing. Both the building inspector's door and the outer door to the assessor's office remained shut. Thinking that someone was in the assessor's office, I walked in and said, "Hi, you people are in early this morning." There was no response and the door to the inner office was locked.

I stood there looking around, and there was a door in the back corner that led you down three steps to a hall where the Brewster Historical Society displayed historical items. I realized that the door was not closed tightly. As I pushed the door open further I made a similar comment, "Gee, you guys are up early." I looked in, and no one was there. I started down the steps and heard the front doors of the hall shut. I looked up and there was nobody there. I walked around and found that nothing had been disturbed. So I went back up the steps and closed the door behind me and let it go at that. A few days later I saw one of the members of the historical society and told him I had found the door open. Shortly thereafter, they nailed the door shut—I don't know if they thought I was going to steal something or what. It wasn't until after I was elected town clerk/treasurer/collector and more substantial experiences took place that I realized that this was probably my first encounter with "my friend."

The next incident took place approximately two weeks after I had taken office. At the end of each day, we closed the vault, closed the windows, shut off the lights, locked the door, and went home. I had a phobia of combination locks and was always convinced that once I spun the lock on the vault I would never get it open again. Around seven o'clock one evening I left home to do a little shopping in town. When I pulled into a store, an old acquaintance pulled up behind me and said, "I was going home to call you. I just drove by the town hall. Do you know that the windows of your office are open and the lights are on? The outside office door is locked. I said something through the window, and no one answered."

I said, "At four-thirty everything was locked up." I immediately got back in the car, drove to the town hall, unlocked an outside door, opened the door to my office, and walked in. Indeed, the windows in my office were open, the lights were on, and the vault door was open. The large safe inside the vault, where we kept all cash and vital records, was still locked.

The following morning I asked the staff if they remembered whether I had closed the vault door and spun the lock the night before. They swore that I had and recalled reassuring me that I would be able to open the vault in the morning. None of the staff had gone back to the office between four-thirty in the afternoon and seven that evening. So that bothered me, but still I didn't put the two separate odd incidents together.

After dinner and on weekends I would often bring my dog, Brewster, back to the office with me. He was a boxer and everyone was afraid of him, but he was gentle. He drooled a lot and would put his head on the laps of selectmen. If they had suit pants on, they didn't appreciate it very much. But I'm a firm believer that if you have a dog and you live alone, you don't leave him alone all the time. He'd rather sleep at your feet than sleep in an empty house. We had a water dish for him, and if the girls worked they fed him.

I remember one night we got down there and I saw what I assumed to be Selectman Fred Kraphol's car in the parking lot and I thought, "What's Fred doing down here at six-thirty? My God, he's never here this early even if there's a night meeting." When I went into the building the outside door was locked and, while that surprised me, I figured that Fred and the people he was meeting had come into the hall. Brewster and I went into my outer office, which had doors both to the selectmen's clerks' office and the selectmen's inner office. Brewster went flying over to the door to the selectmen's inner office and sniffed at the crack under the door where I could see some light. I could also hear voices coming from inside. I could not distinguish what was being said, but I could hear the murmur of various voices. So I told Brewster, "Get away! Get away!" because I figured someone would wonder if we were listening. I took the dog away and told him to lie down. Now, there were tennis courts next door, but we were far enough away that we didn't hear the pop of the ball. Even with the windows open we didn't hear it, and probably even a discussion in the middle of a tennis court, if it carried, wouldn't sound like a conference. This sounded like it was definitely coming from the conference room. It really was words, then pauses, and then it seemed like answers. At least three or four times that evening Brewster got up and went over to that door, and I went over and heard the drone of voices.

At 6:50 P.M. I heard some people talking outside, and I looked out the window to see who was coming into the town hall and saw some people in tennis clothes getting into the car I had thought belonged to Mr. Kraphol. I said to myself, "Wait a minute—if that isn't Fred Kraphol's car, then who's in the selectmen's office?" I could still hear voices in there. As I walked from my desk to the selectmen's office door, I heard two doors open and shut, including the selectmen's outer office door opening into the hallway. I went flying out into the hall, and there wasn't a soul there—no sounds of any outside doors opening and no one in the selectmen's office.

Shortly after this happened all the women who worked at the town hall, including the former town clerk, decided to go out to dinner. We were having a grand time shooting the breeze and finally one of the women said, "There's something I'd like to ask you people, but I don't know how. I don't want you to think that there's something wrong with me."

I said, "Oh, you've heard footsteps and voices, too?"

And she exclaimed, "Thank God, I'm not the only one." Immediately everyone at the table except the previous town clerk started talking at once about different things they had heard. They had all heard banging noises and seemed to think it was coming from upstairs. They'd go up and look and see nothing. When I directly asked the previous town clerk she said, "No comment." She didn't deny it, and she didn't admit it, so I've sometimes wondered if she actually had heard noises and just didn't want to share it.

There were many times when I would be in the town

hall on the weekends or evenings and I would hear the sound of someone walking up and down the stairs, and I would go out and no one would be there. After making a few trips out to look for things, finally I'd go into my own office and lock the door and stay there. I'll never forget this one Saturday morning when the footstep traffic was so pronounced that when I left my office to use the ladies' room, I took the dog with me! It was the only time I was apprehensive. One evening I heard dancing. I also could hear the shuffle of feet upstairs. For about twenty minutes, I heard music. Then it would stop, and people would move around. I recall also hearing scraping noises. The seats they used to have when the upstairs was a meeting hall were fairly long benches with wooden feet. They also had a couple of the same benches in front of the town hall, and people could sit on them. So it was always a very social place. But when you're the only person in the building and hear a whole lot of noise, you know something is going on.

At that time, I never would have suspected Percy Newcomb. I had figured it had to be a former selectman because of all the unexplained activity in the selectmen's office. From what I'd heard, Percy Newcomb was the town clerk for forty-nine years, but I hadn't known that before that he was a selectman. Only after I saw him and described him to a friend did I know it was indeed Percy Newcomb. I was in my office the Saturday morning after the election of 1983 when Larry Doyle, who was quite elderly and had been a selectman in Brewster for a number of terms, was defeated by a guy named Jimmy Crocker and there was tension between the two guys. (Later, they served together as selectmen.) Larry saw my car and came in to see me. The door from my outside office into the selectmen's office was open, as was the door from my office to the hallway. (Often if these two doors were open, the selectmen would walk through my outer office into their office and, on the way by my door, stop and talk.) As Larry and I were talking, I happened to look over his shoulder and thought I saw Jimmy Crocker walk right into the selectmen's office. I thought it was Jimmy because he was short in stature. And he went by kind of fast.

The election had been bitter. Jim wanted to beat Larry because Larry had defeated Jim's grandfather years before. Larry didn't think Jim had what it took to be a selectman and thought that if Jim were elected the town would go to hell in a hand basket. And I thought to myself, "Aw, jeez, Jimmy, what did you come in here today for?" I was thinking the two would get into an argument, which I didn't want to happen in my office because I happened to like both. I wore what must have been a very funny look on my face because Larry asked me what was wrong. I don't remember what I said, but I guess it didn't make much sense to Larry because shortly thereafter he left. As soon as I heard his car door shut, I raced around the corner to the selectmen's office to ask Jim why he came into the office when he had seen Larry's car and knew that Larry was in the building. And there was no one in the office or in the building. The door from the selectmen's office to the hall was closed and locked. From where I was sitting in my office, no one could have gotten out of the selectmen's office without my seeing him or her except through the window, and the windows were locked.

As soon as Larry's car left the driveway, I locked up my office and drove straight to Walter Babbitt's house. Walter was the town hall historian and a great man who instilled in us pride in working for the town. Because of his love of the town and his interest in its history, and because I had told him about each of my previous experiences, I was sure that he could help me identify who it was that I had seen and we were all hearing in the town hall. So when I arrived at his house he said, "Well, quiet down, tell me about it." I don't recall all the details I gave, but I did say that whoever I saw was about Jimmy Crocker's height and build. Walter said, "Oh, you saw Percy Newcomb!"

I immediately said, "No! It can't be Percy, Walter, because he doesn't come in my office. He goes into the selectmen's office and Percy was the town clerk."

Walter said, "He was the town clerk for forty-nine years, but before that he was a selectman. Maybe you're doing all right. Maybe he's happy with what you're doing. Maybe he isn't happy with what the selectmen are doing. I'm sure it was Percy Newcomb."

It wasn't much later that we moved the town hall to a new building. After we moved out, the town started using the building for social events and dances for the elderly. A couple of times, we would visit the building and say, "Well, the ghost ought to be happy now because the house is being used for something good, and it's being used happily."

I don't know what there was about the building. I just had a real feeling for it. Probably the first time I drove by it, I said, "God, that's the ugliest-looking building." But there was just something about it. When I first started working there, right off the bat I had a good feeling. The building was all-wooden with a brick foundation. They've gutted the downstairs and made it beautiful. It's a beautiful building now. What they're using it for is keeping the building alive. In fact, I was the one who came up with the idea of having a celebration for the hundredth anniversary of the town hall.

The town has totally changed in the last few decades. When I was in office, there were many, many things happening in the town. It was growing; it was changing and that might have made him restless. I guess if you love deeply enough and care deeply enough, which I'm sure Mr. Newcomb did in all those years in government, then part of you could go on.

EARNING ITS KEEP

L and's End Inn rests atop Gull Hill in the more residential West End of Provincetown's Commercial Street. Wooden steps wind to the summit, which offers a sweeping view of Cape Cod Bay and the outer arm of the Cape. Benches along the stairway invite guests to enjoy the stillness. A brick walkway travels the grounds, past rustic cedar furniture arranged along the lawn and a Japanese pagoda garden. Rising from a birdbath are sculpted mythological figures. Leering gargoyles and carved hands holding torches serve as outdoor lamps.

The lobby of the massive sixteen-room inn is no less breathtaking, filled with abstract paintings, potted ferns, antique stained glass, and most revealingly, a wide variety of Oriental artifacts and decor. The sheer scope of this huge collection of Far Eastern porcelain, fine art, richly colored carpets, elaborate tapestries, and polished brassware is almost overwhelming to a first-time viewer.

This opulence is the legacy of Captain Charles Higgins, a merchant who built the house before the turn of the century as a personal retreat after a lifetime of world travels acquiring Asian antiques and curiosities.

The object that has received the most attention over the years is the least conspicuous—a small pale green urn that sits by itself high on a wooden shelf above a doorway. The shelf is more than ten feet above the floor, keeping the urn out of reach of staff, guests, visitors, or anyone without a ladder. This is intentional, for the urn is said to bear a curse that brings disaster to anyone who dares touch it. Caution dictates that it can be cleaned only from a distance, with a very long-handled duster.

Current owner Michael MacIntyre doesn't know when the urn first gained its reputation but says it has been part of the inn ever since the place was built. Michael has heard stories of several people over the years who suffered misfortunes after touching the object, including one person who died two weeks after handling it and another individual who subsequently hanged himself in a loft room. Although Michael has had the inn for only a year, he avoids the urn. "I'm not taking it down any time soon," he chuckled. "There's no reason to mess with a curse that has lasted all these years."

ANCIENT SPIRIT

We learned of Nancy Reid's ghost stories from a story in the Cape Cod Register. *The writer, Kathryn Swegart, claimed that during her interview with Nancy, she caught the voice of the ghost on her Sony microcassette recorder.*

Nancy's home is a yellow Queen Anne Victorian with a four-sided tower. She is celebrated as a passionate local historian and author of an exhaustive history of the town of Dennis. She appeared energetic and curious. She had short, bushy, gray hair and warm blue eyes.

As Dan set his tape recorder down, Nancy warned us, with light laughter, that the incident with Kathryn Swegart might occur again.

The sea captain in this house was Captain Roland Kelley. He was my great-uncle. He sailed schooners and went from Bass River with cargoes; then he'd come back with fruit from the Caribbean. The vessel that he had the longest was the *M.E. Elderidge*. He had a fair amount of capital when he built this house, so he really gussied it up. It's quite a spectacular house, really, for South Dennis. And he was very proud of it. He used to have croquet matches on the lawn, and, whenever he'd come home from the Caribbean, he'd have a party and serve fresh fruit. His daughters were very popular, very attractive girls. They went to all the dances and had parties here. So it was a busy house. And he loved his house. So we kind of lean toward our presence being Captain Kelley because it seems as if when exciting things are happening in the family, that's when we notice the noises.

When my daughter was married, we had a reception at the house. At night we'd hear the steps coming down the stairs. And it's really not like just the sounds of a creaky old house. It's regular: bump-bump-bump-bump-bump. People describe it the same way. We had a couple come stay with us—newlyweds. They came down from the guestroom in the morning and said, "Who was banging around all night? We kept hearing these steps on the stairs."

"Oh, well. It must have been Captain Kelley."

We put a light in the tower one Christmas as a decoration. The neighbors said, "Oh, why don't you leave it there? It's nice." We had an awful time with that light. It would be off when we thought it would be on. It would be on when it should have been off. So we went and got a solar timer. It worked for two days, and then it was out. When my two sons went up to see what was wrong, the light had been unplugged. Yet no one remembered going up there and unplugging the light. It isn't as if anyone could just go up there and unplug it. You have to get a ladder and open the trap door and you cannot do it without assistance because there's no stairway you can crawl up. The ladder is kept in the garage. I can't imagine. There's no way anybody could have gotten up there and unplugged that light.

Strange things like that happened. The Kathryn Swegart recording—that really mystified me. I cannot explain that either.

We're in the house alone now. We still have an incident here or there. We've owned the house since 1961. My dad used to visit here a lot when he was a young man. Yes, in fact, he'd been on Captain Kelley's schooner with him. And my cousin, who is still living, remembers coming down here to play croquet and badminton at lawn parties. I don't remember Uncle Roland, although he was still living when I was a little girl.

I'm pretty much convinced it's him, and, when we do anything around the house, it kind of seems as if he comes to see what it is we've done.

I find so many people say, "Oh, you've got a ghost in your house." But, you see, I really don't think of him as a ghost. He's sort of an ancient spirit. He invested so much in this house, and he's still looking out for that investment.

I can only think that, with all of us, we have things that we care about very intensely and are interested in, and we invest an awful lot of our energy in them. Then, when our body is gone, some of that energy is still here. That is kind of what I think is the energy that went into building this house. His personality.

My husband doesn't like to talk about it. But when we have a noisy night, then we speculate a little bit about what Captain Kelley could have been doing.

The chimes clang loudly as the wind picks up. There is a distant rumble of thunder. Gary asks, "Has either of you looked right at the stairs while these noises were coming down?"

No, would you like to try that some night?

She laughs.

No, but one of us did get up once when we heard the noises, but saw no one. And the thing that really is so puzzling to me is, why do we hear the noises coming down the stairs, and no one ever says coming up the stairs? The speculation comes when we both get woken up at night. I've never had the courage to get up with a flashlight. I just sort of lie there and listen. I don't know why.

No one—even the guests—has ever felt that this was something they couldn't put up with. It has never been threatening. Never been threatening.

I don't think he likes the light in the tower.

Not too long ago we were having a woodpecker come every morning and beat on the gutter. We kind of got used to that, and then one time we had all kinds of other noises about three o'clock in the morning. And it had nothing to do with the woodpecker. Nobody else was here except us. We'd been coming here in the summers for so long, and no one had said anything about hearing these things before. We began to wonder why the house was suddenly creaking. And it wasn't creaking. Everyone heard the very same thing. A noise is a noise. You hear a creak in the night, you hear a creak in the night. You hear the wind in the night, you hear a woodpecker, you know what that is.

I'm a pretty practical person, and I just have to say, "Well, I can't understand it. I can't explain it, but there it is." I think I listen with a little less skepticism to other people's experiences. To me, ghost stories—prior to the time we lived in this house—were just ghost stories.

A LITTLE NIGHT MUSIC

*The First Congregational Church of Yarmouth is only
four doors down from Donald and Pat Anderson's cozy
Greek Revival home. However, it's not the source of the pipe
organ music women have heard in the house at night. The
music comes from the Andersons' upstairs bedroom. The
"Old Baker Homestead," as the locals still call it, rests on
historic Route 6A, one of the most scenic stretches of former
sea captains' homes in the United States. The elegant oak
tree in the front yard is what convinced Pat, a nurse in the
O.R. unit at Cape Cod Hospital, to buy the home. The
Andersons refurbished the interior, added antiques, and
changed around the rooms to their liking. Walking around
in socks, Pat first gave us a tour of the cramped but cozy
rooms with low ceilings. Magnet decals from tourist desti-
nations around the States covered her refrigerator in the
kitchen, where she pointed to the minister's closet, where
the Baker family, who first owned the house, may have*

stored the minister's liquor. Moving from room to room, she also described the original layout of the house and where doors used to be. A flintlock hung over the door in the dining room. If one were to write a set of instructions for future ghost authors on how to interview Pat about her ghost, it would read, "No coaxing necessary." Taking a seat in a red director's chair, Pat spoke animatedly with her hands, rarely remaining seated for long. She would jump up to carry out different chores in the kitchen, then quickly return to her seat and continue her entertainingly blunt ghost stories.

I think the main thing about this house is the organ music in the front bedroom that only women hear. Four months after we moved here, I'd hear music at night. I'd wake up and the music would bother me. It was playing right in the room. It's a pretty organ. Not like one of those little things you buy that looks like a piano that everybody rents for the plays and it sounds tinny and everything. It's very nice. Even the chords are nice. It would be chords, or it would be hymns. I'd wake up my husband and say, "Listen to the music."

"What music? I don't hear any music."

"Don, listen to the organ music."

He didn't hear a thing. And he said, "Oh, you're nuts!"

Sometimes it would be so loud I couldn't stand it. I'd come downstairs and read a book for a while and go back in, and there wouldn't be any more music. This would happen maybe once every couple of months, or maybe some nights twice in a row. One day when our son was in the fourth grade and I went to pick him up from school, I said at the office, "Hi, I'm Mrs. Anderson. I'm here to pick up Benjamin."

And the school secretary said, "Oh, you live in the old Baker house!"

"Yes!"

"Doesn't the music drive you crazy?"

"You've heard the music?!"

"My husband was born in that house. But only the women can hear it."

"You're right. My husband cannot hear it."

"Oh, I've heard it. My husband's sister has heard it. My mother-in-law has heard it. All the females would hear it. And it didn't have to be anybody who lived there but just a female who happened to stay in that front bedroom."

"Oh, my God, you know!"

So I came home and told my husband. Before, he didn't believe me, but now he said, "Jeez, maybe somebody across the street's playing the organ."

"There are no lights on in the house across the street. There's nobody who would be playing an organ. They're not playing the organ."

At one point I mentioned it to the people across the street, and they thought, "Isn't that weird?" Now, the bedroom is the original front parlor. The wall consists of three rows of bricks. So, obviously, at one time there must have been an organ in that front room. But it's amazing, because you can pick out some of the songs. The chords drive you nuts.

We're the first people outside of the Baker family to own this house. One section of this house was built around 1808.

The parlor here and the upstairs bedroom were built on Nantucket and dragged over on the ice in 1880. Nantucket Sound used to freeze back then, but now the Gulf Stream keeps it warm. It was easier for the ships to get into Nantucket with the lumber. So it was cheaper to take the lumbermen over to Nantucket and build the house. They would treat it and, if any pieces went through the ice, they could still salvage them, and the timber wouldn't rot. It was funny because when they got it over here, they had mismeasured, so this floor was quite a bit off. You can still see it dips down.

So anyway, between Thanksgiving and Christmas, this door here in the parlor that leads down to the Cape Cod cellar opens. God knows why, but it opens two or three times per day, a few dozen times between those two holidays. Nobody knows who it is who opens the door. Right now I have a vacuum cleaner in front of it because Thanksgiving hasn't come. But I will put nothing in front of that door between Thanksgiving and Christmas. When you're doing your Christmas packing and stuff and you put a big pile of boxes in front of it, it'll tip it over and the door will open. I mean wide open. We've got a rug under it, so it's not like it can open any other way but forcibly. You don't hear it, because it doesn't happen when you're in the room. But you come out and the boxes are on the floor. So you just don't put anything there between Thanksgiving and Christmas. Particularly anything heavy, because I heard once that the person who lived here before me put a china closet there and it would fall over. She'd put it back there, and it would be fine until next year. Then it would fall again. I am not that stupid. I don't put a lock on the door. Because I would not want anything to get upset and break my lampshade.

Different people in the family have tried to figure out who the spirit was who was doing those things. Some thought maybe Christmas was a bad time of year for the spirit. At one time there was an old shed on the property, and Tom Baker used to drive the town hearse, so he had his horse here and he would bring in bodies sometimes, ice them and have them over here.

It's funny because my son never believed when growing up. He'd always heard the story but never paid much attention. But a couple of years ago we had gone off for a few days and he was here. He'd come out of his room to go to work and he'd say, "Oh, my God. The door is open!" He became a believer.

You get used to it. You tell yourself, "It doesn't happen all the time. It doesn't bother me." The organ music, that bothers me. Only because, oh, God, how many times can you listen to "Jesu, Joy of Man's Desiring" again and again? There's no seasonable thing about the organ music. It just comes—sometimes in the dead of summer. The window's wide open. Even with traffic going by, you can hear the organ music. It's like "Boom!" Somebody is playing the music right there. Sometimes I fall back asleep. When I'm awake and reading a book when it starts, I don't mind. Unless it's really loud. Otherwise, if it's soft, it's just like any other classical music on in the background at work in the O.R. It's nice. I went to Sunday School at Federated Church in Hyannis for thirteen years and never missed a Sunday, and I sang in a church choir. So I know quite a few of the pieces. It's always church music.

As you get older, you see there are definitely things that nobody can explain. I'm very open-minded. One of the schoolteachers did a little story. Oh, it was so funny. They came here right near Halloween. It was rainy. It was stormy. I had worked all day. I had a horrible case in the O.R. I didn't know that she was bringing an entire English class here to Mr. and Mrs. Anderson's. So they arrived before me and they all sat around in here. But the funniest thing was when I arrived at the door, I still had my O.R. greens on. I was covered with blood. And here they were to talk about Mrs. Anderson's ghost in her house. Oh, they loved it!

They had questions made out for me. They all had to look at the door. We opened the door, and they had to be guaranteed there was nothing there. Oh, they just loved that stuff.

MAGNETISM

The undisputed queen of Cape Cod's haunted buildings, the Barnstable House on Old Kings Highway has been the setting for countless ghost experiences over the years. Its name was often the first to pop up in response when we told locals about the subject of our book.

The meticulously restored former restaurant, with twelve-over-twelve sash windows typical of the Colonial period, currently houses a developer, designer, and marketer of telephony switches. Séances inside were said to have revealed the presence of at least eleven different ghosts, though in the opinion of one former employee with whom we spoke, "The building itself was the spirit."

Consistent versions of its stories are difficult to come by, as accounts vary from one person to the next. Even the year of the house's construction is in dispute. Some sources say 1716 (the date on the foremost chimney), from timbers cut two years earlier; others claim it was dismantled at another location and brought to the Cape by barge in 1715. Perhaps the hardest details to establish are those concerning the most notorious story associated with the timeworn structure – that of four firemen who were part of a group that responded to an alarm call there sometime in the early '70s. The four men claimed to have seen a mysterious young lady in a white dress on the premises. One of the firemen told us that the long, flowing garment she wore was typical attire for a young woman in the counterculture era, and that she was probably just one of many onlookers whose presence on the grounds was due to curiosity about what the fire department was doing on the property. This prosaic explanation notwithstanding, the story became something of a local legend over the years, spawning several variations. In the most flamboyant version, the young woman is standing in an upstairs window surrounded by flames, whereupon she floats safely to the ground and promptly disappears.

Constance Mack, a waitress at the former restaurant from 1980 to 1982, stated that one of the men present that night told her that while talking to the woman in question, he happened to look down and saw that she had no feet!

Constance, a dark-haired woman with expressive brown eyes, told us she never saw a spirit during her tenure at the Barnstable House, but there were always "sensations" in her peripheral vision. "It would be as if somebody had just walked by you," she said. "You would look, and there would be nothing there. That happened on a regular basis."

She and her coworkers would feel sensations of cold wind. Lots of staff heard footsteps, saw doorknobs turning

in the attic rooms upstairs, and heard a child crying. They
wondered if the child was a ten-year-old girl named Lucy
who was said to have drowned long ago in an underground
spring beneath the building. Despite the activity—and
partly because of it—Constance describes her years in the
inn with affection.

T he incident of a glass shattering against a wall was
the most dramatic thing I ever saw. It was a slow
night, probably wintertime. As you came into the building,
there was a really nice lobby—like a hotel lobby—with a
fireplace. A glass of water was sitting on the lobby counter
when, all of a sudden, it flew across the room. It splashed
against the wall, and the glass broke.

We had heard of similar incidents in the bar. It was very
rustic back there with rough-hewn walls and beams. The
floors were crooked. Part of it used to be stables. And the
bartenders talked about glasses popping off of the bar all
the time.

I think that kind of stuff happens a lot. You question it,
because it doesn't fit into our scope of what reality is. You
want to make it fit somehow. So you come up with a logical explanation for it. Perhaps someone—or even I—may
have accidentally sent the glass airborne with a swipe of
the hand, but I'm not so sure.

The owner of the restaurant was very open about the
unusual goings-on. He held séances in the building and
really promoted that whole aspect of it. Spirits revealed
their identities to the psychics presiding over these séances.
All of the spirits were friendly. One was a woman who

liked the color blue. Consequently, the owner painted a small reception room blue.

The ghosts really liked all of the stuff going on there. I think they hung around because it was a fun place to be. We had great Halloween costume parties with a coffin in the lobby. We did a lot of weddings. It was a creative place to work.

The staff got along like family. I don't feel it was an accident that we all wound up there working together. I think all of us had some interest in spirituality. And we talked about that a lot. More of us believed in that stuff than in a normal work situation.

I consider myself open to those kinds of phenomena anyway. My personal feeling is that most ghosts are people who just don't want to completely leave this earthly, physical space that we're in. I believed that anything could be possible in that building.

And it was a beautiful building. The people who did the work on it really had an appreciation for older homes. It wasn't elaborate, but it was cozy and special. People are definitely drawn to the building. People that I waited on have said they were driving by the building with no intention of stopping to eat or anything like that. But they would come back for lunch and stay the whole afternoon. They had no idea why. I think people just felt really good there.

It's a romantic place. We always had the fireplace going. I remember one year, around Valentine's Day, we hired a harp player. She had a red, sequined evening gown. We turned off almost all the lights and just had candlelight. And it snowed. There were a lot of moments like that. One summer day we had a piano recital. We had an old grand piano. And the owner's wife had made a bouquet with all the wildflowers. The curtains would blow, and you could smell the sweets and the flowers. It was like out of a time gone by.

Barnstable House is a throwback to that era. Barnstable Village is a really tight-knit community. It's like the old Cape used to be. People walk down to the store or hang out at the little coffee shop. And they ate at the Barnstable House, which was a restaurant for many years. I think they all felt loyal to it. There was no central heating. We would heat with a coal stove and kerosene heaters in the wintertime. People would sit there with their mink coats on, eating twenty-five-dollar dinners. I mean, people don't do that!

I feel privileged that I worked there and that I had that building in my life.

TREASURE

Among the objects dug up in the backyard of Bob Lavery's full Cape in Barnstable were a gold mourning ring, a Spanish piece of eight, seventeenth-century marbles, and a six-foot-tall clay cistern. But the discovery that impressed him the most may have occurred in his living room.

Bob is a painter and a retired schoolteacher of art and art history. Years back he was a representative painter, but he soon gravitated to the abstract style, which he felt gave him more freedom of interpretation. "I try to strike an emotion out of the viewer to get them to feel something about my work," he said. "I teach the same approach to my students. I encourage critical thinking rather than imitation or working with the non-thinking side of their brain. So they're taking everything they know and putting it into something visual."

No doubt his sensitivity to the visual underlies his fondness for unusual and well-rendered historical treasures. On display in his house are conversation pieces ranging from Walt Disney memorabilia to a Japanese porcelain statuette of

Hotai, a smiling "happy god" who is said to bring good luck when you rub his belly. A double-cross-constructed front door leads into the parlor. In the Colonial period, the crosses were intended to drive away witches and other evils. Rosehead nails peek out of the floorboards in the sitting parlor. Built in 1639, the home originally served as a malt house. In the cellar are the remains of three beehive ovens used to cure the hops. A small stream running under the driveway may have turned a water wheel to grind the barley.

I rented this house for four years, and then we bought it and started some major restoration. In the 1970s it became the in thing to do—to buy an old house and refurbish it. I've put a lot of work into the place. At this point it's a pretty tight little old house.

We had owned the house maybe three years. One evening my wife, Pat, had gone to bed upstairs. I was watching TV on the living room couch when I suddenly had the feeling that somebody was watching me. I looked up and saw a woman right in this hallway. She was short and stout—probably around five feet three inches tall. She had a round face with her hair pulled back and wore glasses and one of those large pinafore-type aprons. Just from being an antique buff, I knew her clothes were from around 1850. I saw her for maybe five seconds. Then she dissipated. I didn't think anything of it. I didn't even mention it. I thought maybe I was hallucinating. But I thought it was curious that it lasted so long.

About one month later, I had a fire going in the other front room. I was sitting in there just relaxing and enjoying life. I was watching the fire slow down, because you don't go to bed with a fire going. All of a sudden I had the same feeling that somebody was watching me. I looked and saw the same person. I mean, I really could look at her. She wasn't opaque—she was like a hologram. It was a lady in her work clothes—dark gingham, tight collar, glasses, and so forth. She wasn't creepy, just passive and very observant. It was a nice experience. She was just looking at me and I was going crazy, because as a young man reading Shakespeare and stuff, I'd read about people in the Middle Ages speaking to ghosts in Latin. They were learned ghosts back then. Anyhow, I was trying to think of the words in Latin to speak. Of course, why would she speak Latin? Because she was obviously American. But I was sitting there trying to figure out how you should speak, and by the time everything was coming to me, she went away again. That time I did tell my wife, Pat, about it. My wife is really a very practical person— a really straight arrow. She didn't think anything of it.

A couple of months after that episode, Al Pearson, a friend who I was teaching with at Dennis-Yarmouth High School, came over. We'd had a meeting in school and he came home with me. I sat in the red chair, and he was on the couch. We were just shooting the breeze, and I made us a couple of Bloody Marys. We hadn't even started drinking them yet. My wife came in and said, "I'm going to bed, so I'll see you later on." Al and I continued talking. I was looking at him and he was looking at me. And she came into the room. This time she was moving. The lady came maybe a foot and a half into the room—just enough that it interrupted both of our visions then just disappeared. And Al said, "What was that?"

I said, "Well, I think it's something I've been seeing around here."

"No, it was Pat."

"No, it's not Pat. She's in bed."

He got up, walked down the hall, and called up the stairs. Sure enough, my wife was in bed. He came back and said, "I don't believe this."

I said, "Well, believe it, because I've seen it twice."

"Will she come back?"

"Well, I don't know. She usually shows up when you don't expect her."

Al stayed until two in the morning waiting in vain for her to come back.

I once had a babysitter here who thought my wife and I were coming home because she had seen something moving up the hall. When she saw that it wasn't us she thought there was an intruder in the house. She was on the phone with the police when we came home. She was positive somebody was in the house.

My wife doesn't believe in this kind of stuff. Yet she would be sitting on the couch at night and would hear someone walking across the ceiling, stop, and resume from back where it started—a steady thump, thump, thump. Of course she knew no one was up there, because the kids would be in bed. But she heard those sounds several times.

The only time I felt a little bit threatened was when my daughter Sarah was about two. She'd woken up just before dawn, and she came into our bedroom upstairs. She was playing at the foot of our bed. She woke me up. So I picked her up, and I said, "Well, hey, hey, it's kind of early to be up." I carried her back into her bedroom and put her in her crib. I got back into bed and was just going to sleep again when there was a really violent kicking, like someone with a heavy boot kicking the bed. Something was banging and making that bed move. I thought it was Sarah. I said, "Didn't I tell you. . .," looked for her, and climbed out of my bed because I thought she might have gotten under the bed. She was asleep in her crib. I came back to the bed and I asked my wife, "Did you feel that?"

She said, "Yes, I did. What was it?"

"I don't know what it was!"

That kicking took a certain amount of strength. Since then, everything has been fine. Twenty-two years of peace and quiet. If I hadn't seen the same apparition two and a half times, I would say that it wasn't a reality. But I know I saw what I saw.

Being a Roman Catholic, I know that everyone dies and goes to Heaven and some people go to Purgatory. In the Middle Ages they thought that all the spirits wandered. If we feel souls go somewhere, then why not? I'm glad I experienced it. I consider myself lucky.

My father won't even stay in my house. He won't sleep here. He woke up one night with the hair standing up on his arms. He didn't know what it was, but something brushed by his arm and woke him. He doesn't even want to talk about it. My kid brother told me, "He doesn't like staying at your house at night." I've never felt threatened, other than the banging against my bed. So that's the extent of my experiences. Yeah, I wouldn't mind if it came back. I'd like to reaffirm it.

PASSAGES

*Michelle Kerr, a forty-two-year-old emergency dispatcher
with the Barnstable County Sheriff's Office, describes herself
as intuitive, open-minded, and approachable. And she feels it
is exactly those qualities that enable her to have encounters
with kindred spirits. The bulk of her experiences have
occurred at her family homestead, a majestic, rambling three-
hundred-year-old house on Mill Way in Barnstable, across the
street from historic Cobb's Hill Cemetery. The house interior
is quirky and quaint, full of uneven door frames, glass doorknobs, crooked floors, twenty-seven-inch wide floorboards,
haphazard bends in the hallways, and steep staircases. The
basement houses an antique printing press that the
Smithsonian Institution has made inquiries into purchasing.*

    *Michelle shared her stories and her infectious enthusi-
asm for her family history at the former Shirdan's
Country Kitchen in Hyannis. She came across as friendly
and alert. She had long, tousled dark hair and was wear-*

*ing a light blue jacket, indigo jeans, and black boots. She
cautiously asked questions at first about the nature of our
book, but it wasn't long before she became talkative and
open, her dark eyes communicating the playful mood of
her stories. She confided in us like old friends.
Occasionally she punctuated a sentence with a hearty,
good-natured laugh.*

There's a kindred spirit at my house. He's a great guy.
My home is a family property. My great-uncle Harry
and my great-uncle Andrew bought it in 1920, although the
first part of the house was built in the 1600s. It's a beautiful old house. It used to have twenty-two rooms for a single family. My father owns it now, and he has converted it
into apartments.

I moved into the house in 1988. I had the first floor, which
was six or seven rooms. My father renovated it for me when
I moved in. The spirit in the home walked upstairs and
downstairs. It sounded like someone pacing the perimeter
of the rooms, checking them out. I had known there was a
spirit there for a long time because of what happened to my
brother one night (when he lived there in the early 1980s).
My family members were sitting in the living room when
the wooden chair my younger brother was in tilted back on
its two hind legs. His feet were not touching the floor. He
was just kind of balanced there, very precariously. He had
goose bumps all over his body, and all the hair on his legs
stood up. Then he came down.

My youngest sister and my brother's girlfriend saw this
happen, and they asked him, "What just happened to you?"

He said it was the strangest sensation that he had felt in his life. It was as if warm water had just flushed through his body, almost like a current.

His girlfriend said she woke up at night to a man's face floating over her. He had a bewildered look on his face, as if he were trying to figure out who she was. He had gray hair and a beard. She feels she was awake. It wasn't like she was asleep.

So I'd known this was happening for years. A few years ago, a couple of old friends and I were sitting in the living room of the house when we heard somebody walking around in my parents' apartment, which is upstairs. My parents had the second and third floors, but they're only there for the summer months and for Christmas because they live in Florida now. So the house is empty. And this sea captain spirit was walking around—we heard him. My friends said, "Who's gone upstairs?" And I went upstairs, but I knew who it was. I've never been frightened of him, although most women in the house would get very uncomfortable. I'm not afraid of spirits at all because I have very strong religious beliefs, so I feel that keeps me safe.

I had a group of women over one night. We were all sitting in the living room, and one of my friends was telling a story. All of a sudden we heard this little voice say, "Whew! Are you done yet?"

And everybody in the room went, "Who said that?" "Where did that come from?"

Since I knew what it was, I said, "I know you guys will probably think I'm a little crazy here, but I have a sea captain's spirit in this house."

They couldn't believe me, but they all swore they heard it. They all described hearing the exact same thing.

I sensed that the spirit was really content when I moved in because I decorated the house in the Old Victorian style with a lot of antiques from the late 1800s that had been in the family. I actually had gas lanterns, brass hooks, and things from the era when he was around. I think he used to rent a room here when he came into port. There was another sea captain who lived in the house, but I don't think he's the spirit. There's also a woman spirit. I'm not entirely sure who she is.

I also have had an experience across the street in Cobb's Hill Cemetery. It was the year that disc cameras came out. My sister-in-law's brother had just purchased a camera, and he was taking pictures of us one night. We decided to go into the cemetery and we brought the camera. There were about seven or eight of us. It was an eerie night. The clouds were blowing through the sky, and there was a full moon. It was eerie, but it was calm—very serene. The camera wouldn't work in the cemetery at all. It did work later when we were back in the house. So we were walking around, and my family was aware that I have this sensitivity—as does my mother, as did my grandmother. And they said, "Michelle, do you feel anything?"

I said, "Well, no, not really. Why?"

And they said, "Could you see if you do?"

I said, "Sure." So I said, "If there's anything around that would like to make contact with me. . . ." Then I invoked the Lord's Prayer, which is what I usually say when I invoke the spirits. Then, all of a sudden, I felt this thing grab my ankle. It was pitch-black, other than when the clouds let a little bit of moon shine through. I mean you could see shadows, but nothing clearly defined. So, when I felt something grab my ankle, I looked down and I said, "What the hell is that?" And I saw this girl's face, with her hand reaching up. She had brown eyes and dark brown hair—very plain-looking. And looking like, "Help me." All I could get is this sense that she was unhappy, that something tragic happened, and that she wasn't at rest. It was almost pitch dark. The ground and her features were opaque. All I could see clearly were her face and her hand—not her neck or anything else. And she was calling for help—like she was in a place where she wasn't at rest.

I work in the sheriff's department as an emergency fire and rescue and police dispatcher, so I tend to pay attention to what's going on around me. Right then I got a bad sense in the total dark of the cemetery—I don't know how to say it because it's too much of a cliché—and looked and saw a dark shadowy presence nearby. I felt very threatened by it. I said to everyone, "I would like to leave now, and I am going to leave now. You guys can stay if you want." Then I just walked around the hill and into the house.

My son marked the spot with a rock, and the next day he went over with my niece—they were like twelve and eleven at the time—and wrote down exactly what the gravestone said. It was the grave of a young girl. I looked up her record in the town registry, and it said that she had died in a horse and buggy accident.

Getting back to the house, I've had my things moved in it. When you live alone, you know what you move and

what you don't move. I'm very habitual. I tend to put
things back where they go all the time, so I always know
where they are. But I would come home and find things
broken. I had plants tipped over. I don't have pets. There's
no reason that should have happened. The house was three
hundred years old, so it wasn't settling. As it was, some of
the floors were crooked.

It's a great old house. There are windows in clothes
closets. There are stairways all over the place that are
closed off now. And this is where the spirit goes. He only
stays in the front part of the house. He always stays by the
fireplaces.

I don't actually know if Great Uncle Andrew and Great
Uncle Harry ever sensed the ghost. They were very, very
strange people. The Kerrs were always brilliant people but,
I think, very eccentric. I guess we all are eccentric. I speak for
myself, too. The Kerrs distance themselves from negative
thoughts and go along with nature and do their own thing.
Harry was a staunch extremist who went to MIT. He owned
a printing press that he kept in the basement. I guess he was
about ninety-four when he stopped printing. He had these
huge magnifying glasses that he used to wear and he was
all hunched over. Harry was also one of the founders of the
Barnstable Fire Department in the 1920s. My great-aunt was
the first female doctor at the women and children's hospital in Boston. Women didn't even vote back then, but she
earned her medical degree at the University of Edinburgh in
Scotland. My uncle Clyde owned an almond orchard. Just
really strange people. I don't know if they had any contact
with any of the spirits that live there.

There are actually two spirits. Over the last few years I've been aware of a second. She is very sweet-smelling. Have you smelled an old lady's old-type perfume that's so heavy when you walk by it almost gags you? I would always know when she was there. In the five or six years I have lived there, she has only come out a few times, always in my bedroom.

There are a lot of people who don't know that I have these stories. If you go out spouting this off to people, they think you're nuts. They'll want to take you away in a straitjacket for twenty days' observation. And I've always had things happen to me. I've always sensed things. I've always known things. When my grandmother passed away, I looked right at my mother. I was driving in a car. And I looked at my mother and said, "Mum, Gramma just died."

She looked at me and said, "What?"

I said, "Gramma just died."

Oh, my God, she was panic-stricken because her mother was in the hospital. When we got home and pulled in the driveway, the phone was ringing. It was the next door neighbor up there at my grandmother's house. And she told me that my grandmother had passed away.

That kind of thing has always happened to me. I just see a flash or something. It's not like I go into a coma or stupor. I don't have seizures. I don't suffer from any mental disorders—other than being eccentric, I guess, or flamboyant. I just have a visual flash, nothing you could probably even register. I have mixed feelings about it. When I saw that very dark form on the top of the hill in the cemetery, that scared me. And that's when I left. Before, when I saw the girl grab my ankle, I wasn't frightened. I just felt sad. I felt sorry that she wasn't in either world and that she wasn't at peace. When you pass from one world to the next, you should go in peace.

THE SPIRIT OF OSTERVILLE

The first qualities that come to mind when many Cape Codders think of Osterville is that it's quiet and isolated. Route 28 does not pass through the center of Osterville so, if you're heading into town, you're usually going there with a purpose.

Unlike other spots on the Cape that cater more to tourists, everything in Osterville seems to be done with residents in mind. The downtown area is uncongested, trim, and proper with a small park with sculpted gardens and a "Museum Complex" that holds five buildings of the Osterville Historical Society. The town has longstanding businesses like Wimpy's Restaurant and upscale shops like Gone Chocolate and Oak & Ivory. Absent are the boutiques for tourists and cookie-cutter chain stores. Most of the businesses in Osterville are on the eastern side of the street, and most of the residences are on the western side. Along Main Street some of the homes and businesses are elegant and have character, but some houses are set so far back from the road that all one sees are the driveways; in this respect, the town resembles rural communities in western Massachusetts.

Bob Harmon says that Osterville also has a lot of supposedly haunted houses. He suspects it's partially because of the high number of older buildings and partially because of the town's seafaring background, which carried with it a lot of folklore. Many of the homes that had a reputation for being haunted were big houses that fell into disrepair when homeowners decided to stay in the Hamptons rather than come back for the summer. One of the more infamous was a house set far back off Main Street with a really long narrow driveway and an enormous beech tree in the front yard and wisteria everywhere. Three houses down by the boatyard also were labeled as "haunted," as was a building that was torn down next to Swift's Market. But the only ghostly encounter that Bob ever had was in the 707 Building, which was diagonally across from Swift's. Half hidden from Main Street, the no-frills building was once home to a sea captain, but now is a mixed-use building with apartments and commercial space.

Bob, now a sculptor, sat down to share his story. He had dark hair with curly front bangs and a full beard and a curious, wide-eyed expression. After joking about tossing his dog (and catching it), photographing it in mid-air and generously offering it to us as a book cover for a work called "The Floating Dog," Bob described his unusual encounter.

At the time of my incident, in the late 1970s, the 707 Building just held offices, not apartments. I was cleaning carpets at eight thirty or nine o'clock at night.

These carpet cleaners came with really tremendously long cords, over fifty feet of cord. So I was in the third room from where the machine was originally plugged in. And there was a really loud thump. Almost like upstairs four or five people had jumped up and then landed simultaneously. It was really loud—percussive throughout the house. So I shut my machine off and froze, because I knew for a fact I was the only one in the building. And I thought that was certainly a good reason to take an inventory of what was going on in the building.

We had heard stories growing up, because the building was just down the street from my home. We knew a family that lived there quite well. They had had some things happen. Sort of poltergeist kind of stuff—things falling or moving. I remember them telling stories about doing dishes or something like that and having a plate fly off the shelf and break. There used to be a hairdresser's shop in the bottom floor called Carmen's. It's not there any longer. It's just an apartment now. But they used to swear the house was haunted and all kinds of things would happen to them. Red water used to come in through the attic window. But nobody knew what was actually happening because the window itself was nailed shut and the floor was completely dry underneath the window.

I'd never had an experience before and can't say I was too primed for one that night. But there was this really loud noise that shook everything, and I stopped. So I poked my head around the corner of the stairs to the second floor, and I sort of just stopped and listened, and I heard no more sounds or anything. I walked halfway up the stairs again and listened, and there was nothing. So I went back to my machine, and I went to turn it on just to start working again, and it wouldn't go on. So I followed the cord back to that other room thinking it had unplugged itself, but it was plugged in. I tried switching it on again, and it still wasn't working. So, at that point, I guess I started to think that I might have blown a fuse and the noise was associated with the electricity in the building. So I went into the basement, where the panel is. It's just a Cape Cod basement with a dirt floor and some stone foundation. There were circuit breakers, not fuses. And they were all fine. So I went back upstairs to make sure the cord was in properly, and the cord was out. I hadn't unplugged it. So then I plugged it back in, went back out, and the machine worked fine. I finished that room, and I had the hallway with the stairwell to do last.

I remember getting stung with a little bit of nervousness, because I couldn't understand how the cord had just been unplugged earlier. It was out at least three feet from the wall. And I think that's what sort of got me thinking that there was some kind of strange thing going on. So I called my friend Gordon, who lives just down the street. I said, "Come up and hang with me while I finish this thing and I'll grab everything up and we'll leave." So he came up. I told him what was going on, and we wrapped up. Everything worked terrifically. I told him about the thump and everything. And he went upstairs while I was working, because he would do that kind of thing. He didn't see anything out of the ordinary. We packed up. We were going to leave, and as I was locking the door, I heard someone exhale. So I stopped. And I said, "Gordon, did you hear that?" And he said, "No." I said, "Come inside with me." So we went up again. Halfway up the stairs, he said, "I didn't hear anything," and he turned and left. And that's when I still to this day swear to God that I heard breathing. It was very clear, very steady—inhale and exhale, inhale and exhale—at the top of the stairs. Almost like breathing for a doctor, when you have to inhale deeply and exhale.

That was enough for me. I just left. I locked up, went outside and said, "Gordon, I could have sworn I heard breathing at the top of the stairs." And he wouldn't entertain that at all. He had been upstairs, and it was getting late. I'm trying to remember why we didn't do the Nancy Drew thing. I think it was probably ten or ten thirty, and the job was done. I think it was basically because we had much more interesting things to do, given that we were eighteen years old and it was a weekend night. And that was it.

But it was just as clear as anything I've ever heard. I think anybody just sort of wonders about this kind of thing until something unexplainable happens. Nothing like that has ever happened to me since then.

THE BAD-LUCK BABYSITTER

Another association that Cape Codders have with Osterville is that it is affluent, but this phenomenon is recent. The name "Osterville" derives from "Oyster Village." Although the Crosby family has a booming boat-building business that stretches back as far as 1798, the village thrived for over a century on the productive oyster flats in and around Grand Island and Little Island. Fishermen still farm the flats to this day, but the livelihood of the village dramatically changed with the influx of summer inhabitants. One of the most telling indications is that the islands now make up Oyster Harbors, a posh gated community with its own private golf course and the highest percentage of lawn jockeys on the Cape.

The coastline in general along Osterville is noteworthy. Samson Island, an uninhabited barrier island just south of Grand Island, is thought by some to be the home of the departed soul of Hannah Screecham, a rumored witch who the pirate Blackbeard may have trusted to guard his buried

*treasure. Legend has it that Hannah used to be seen on the
island dancing, casting spells, and boiling magic potions.*

*Dowses Beach, on the easternmost spit of land jutting
out into Nantucket Sound, offers a panoramic view of
Craigville Beach and Hyannisport. Seaview Avenue, which
runs along private shoreline from Crystal Lake to Osterville
Point, has a rural feel with wooded driveways designated
"private" branching off the road. There's new construction
going on, but many homes on Seaview are of older vintage
than the sprawling mansions on the islands. Most are also
more modest, one of the exceptions being a home where
Claire Hogan had a baffling experience twenty-five years
ago as a freshman in high school.*

I was babysitting in this huge house right on the water.
My father was caretaker for the property. So we subsequently became babysitters. It was just a gorgeous house.
It was like a small mansion, with at least seven or eight
bedrooms and probably four or five baths. There was a
music room, a big formal dining room, a huge formal living room, and a foyer. And it was way back from the
road—a quarter mile back from the road. The caretaker's
cottage was out front. That's what they called it. The caretaker didn't live there. It was like a two-bedroom house.
They rented it out, or one of their kids stayed there. It was
a really beautiful house.

It was pouring rain that night, and I was watching TV
and talking on the phone to my then-boyfriend, now my
husband. I was in the music room, which was so named
because it had a great big grand piano and there were four
or five sliding glass doors all along the wall, with long cur-

tains in front of them, that looked right out on the ocean. I was just sitting there, watching TV and talking on the phone with Chip, and all of a sudden all of the sliding glass doors slid open at the same time, and the curtains started blowing in. They weren't electric or hooked up to open all at once. In fact, you really had to put a little muscle behind it to open them. I can't imagine them sliding open periodically because they were loose or anything.

I got really afraid and threw the phone down on the couch and ran through two other rooms around the corner into the kitchen. Now, from the kitchen I could see the back stairs and the front stairs. The kids I was taking care of were around age three and were both in the bedrooms upstairs. So I could tell they hadn't come down, which was my main concern. I was afraid they would come down and something bad would happen to them.

So I picked up the phone extension in the kitchen, and I said, "Something strange is going on. All the doors slid open. The wind is blowing." I was really afraid. And as I was talking to Chip on the phone, something was picking up the receiver and hanging it up, then taking it off and hanging it up, then taking it off. You could hear it clicking in the other room so I was afraid somebody was in the house. I asked Chip if he would have somebody go across the street to his grandmother's house and call my parents because I was afraid for him or me to hang up the phone. I just wanted to maintain some connection to outside the house. I was afraid if I hung up I'd never be seen again or who knows what. So, his mother went across the street, called my parents, and told them that something strange was happening and would they please come to get me. She got back on the phone with me and said, "Just get a butcher knife and stay watching the stairs so you can keep an eye on the kids and wait for your father to come." That's what I did, basically. I just sat there with my little butcher knife and my phone. The next fifteen minutes I just remember being on the phone and talking back and forth to people on the other end. I still would hear the clicking of the phone, but that's the only thing I heard. I couldn't see the music room to see what was happening to that phone. I could only see the stairs to make sure the kids didn't come down.

Then, all of a sudden, there was a knock at the door and I had to walk down this long hall. I mean, it was almost like something you'd see in a horror movie—with all these closed doors on either side. I had the knife, and I was walking down the hall, and I opened the door, and there was my father, and I all but leaped into his arms.

I was hysterical, crying, because I was just so terrified. We went into the music room and the phone was back on the hook, and all the doors were slid shut again like I'd never been in there. I said, "I'm never babysitting here again. Ever."

I didn't for many, many years. Then when I was about twenty, they asked me if I would sit just once more, and because it was during the day I said I would. This was not supernatural at all. I was sitting there minding my own business and all of a sudden, I heard, "Come out with your hands up!"

She laughs.

Unbeknownst to me, one of the brothers had come home, and he had accidentally set off the silent alarm and went down in the basement to shut it off. The house was so huge, I didn't even know he was in the basement. I opened the door, and there were all these cruisers with their guns pointing at the door, and I was saying, "I'm the babysitter! I'm the babysitter! Please don't shoot me!" So I said, "That's it. I'm done." I never went back after that.

CREEPY COTTAGE

Claire also shared her stories about her former home on Great Marsh Road in Centerville.

My husband and I moved into a tiny little house. It was like a doll cottage. Weird things used to happen in that house all the time. We found a very old gravestone in the backyard. It wasn't standing. It was in the dirt, underneath leaves and things like that. We tried to match it up with some of the local cemeteries, but we never could. You could see the first three or four letters of a woman's name, and 1807 was the date on it. I don't even know if it has anything to do with the property or not. But I remember finding that in the backyard.

We had a dog at the time named Baron, who was just a black mutt that we got from the SPCA, and he used to wake up at around two o'clock every night and bark at the closet.

She laughs.

It was very strange. He just barked at the closet. His

hackles would rise, and he didn't like whatever was in there. A car hit him shortly thereafter. While we were away, he got loose and was hit.

But the weirdest thing that ever happened in that house was that I was working eleven to seven at Centerville Nursing Home, and my husband also worked the night shift at Polaroid in New Bedford. I had come home from work. This is when it was just my husband and me. The dog had already been killed, and we didn't have any other pets. And all the doors and windows were locked from the inside, not from the outside, which is how I locked them when I'd left. I had to break a window to get in.

One day I got up and came downstairs, and there was this red stuff all over the wall. It was dripping down from the ceiling all over the wall. It didn't look like blood or anything. But it was definitely like a rust-red liquid. Every day we'd get up and come downstairs and it would be there. It would drip down all over the backdoor, all over the doorknobs. There was this little square above it that looked like somebody had hammered it on to cover a hole in the ceiling. We took that down and went up and looked around in the floor up there, but we didn't see anything.

It only dripped for a couple of weeks. Then it never did it again. We lived there for about a year, and I don't remember what time of year it happened. But it wasn't raining. That was a creepy house. It was very creepy. We'd just wash off the red stuff every day. When you got up the next day, it would be all over the walls again. We were afraid that the landlord had stuck a body up in the ceiling or something like that. But we never found anything.

The other thing that used to happen is we'd be watching TV and the channels would change. It was before you had remotes. We used to have this tiny, tiny little TV. The knob would flick, and the channels would change. Other people experienced that, too. Kathleen, who used to work at the nursing home, came over one day and was watching TV and saw it flick. That was a very strange house. I was very happy to move out.

CAPTAIN'S KISS

Molly Murphy recalled encountering the ghost she refers to as "the captain" while she was staying in an old Victorian house on Upper County Road in Dennis with her husband, Steve. Molly, a spry bartender with curious brown eyes, had gone to bed after returning from an evening out.

I was awakened by someone kissing my cheek. I thought it was Steve. I looked over, and he had his back to me. He was under the covers snoring like a buzz saw. I couldn't move him. I looked back up, and there was a face over my face. It was an older man, a white-bearded man. No body, just a face. He looked like a typical sea captain, except he didn't have on a hat. He wasn't smiling when I first saw him. But when I realized what I was looking at, that was when he smiled. And it was very calming. It was very serene. I wasn't spooked at all. I knew I wasn't afraid of him. It was like there was an air of calm in the whole room. I thought, "Well, I think he likes me."

There were stories that the daughter of the former owner of the house used to get up and say that an old man was playing with her all night long, and that's why she was so tired in the morning.

But the kiss was what blew me away. I wouldn't have expected it to feel so physical. He had a gorgeous smile. He was a handsome, handsome man. I was impressed by how good-looking he was. He just smiled and disappeared in the blink of an eye. I waited for him to come back, saying, "Come back, come back." They don't come on command, apparently.

A MOMENT IN TIME

The story of the "Freeze Men" is so unusual and different that few who've heard it have known what to make of it. "It was really weird," said Randy Wickersham, manager of Spinnaker CD in Hyannis, recalling the experience his mother and her friend had one late spring day in the early '70s. "One of the strangest aspects of the story," Randy said, "is that no one ever talked about it."

Randy, tall and slim with an irreverent sense of humor, occasionally laughed as he related the incident but admitted that, at the time, it had strongly affected him. He had been about ten years old and living on Kent Lane in Hyannis when he joined his mother, his best friend, Dave, and Dave's older sister, Rita, on a drive looking for yard sales. In his family, yard sales were a big thing. Randy explained that Rita was at least ten years older than he and Dave. "Younger than my mother, but sort of in that middle period where she could be friends with your mother but never hang out with you or your friends."

Their drive eventually took them down by the Ocean Street docks in Hyannis, which, Randy remembered, "weren't as built up as they are now." He recalled sizable wooded areas and seeing the occasional weather-beaten shack near the shore. His mother had seen a sign, for either an estate sale or a yard sale. They turned onto the dirt road, thickly lined on either side with pine trees, that led to a small house.

"You couldn't see the whole area," said Randy, "but there was nothing else on that road. So I assumed it was a driveway up to the house. Although this had to be the house indicated by the sign, the building was very beaten up and more like a large utility shed of the type used to store boats. It had almost all of the appearance of a house in terms of shingling and windows." Randy's mother thought it was a garage and guessed there was a garage sale. Randy was talking with Dave, and the boys weren't really paying attention to the front-seat conversation. The women decided to leave the car to look around, since there were no other people or cars to be seen.

"I remember them going in different directions," said Randy, "each one taking a different side of the house, going around the perimeter to see if there was stuff set out. Less than two or three minutes passed before they both came back, and they had really emotionless faces. Almost like they were in a trance. They got in the car. I knew something bothered them because they didn't talk. Normally when those two were together they'd be very talkative—they'd comment on what they saw, what they got. And there was dead silence, which made me pay attention. I remember looking at Dave, and he knew something wasn't right, too. You could just tell.

"I didn't think somebody yelled at my mom for being on their property," said Randy, "or that there was a dog tied up and it jumped at them, because in either of those situations I think the conversation level probably would have increased. It would be something to talk about.

"I remember leaning up front between the seats and saying, 'What did you see?' And my mother said, 'I don't want to talk about it. I just want to get out of here.' And the way she said it . . . . My mother wasn't a dramatic person."

Randy remembers going directly home. Dave and Rita lived next door to Randy and his mom, and during the ten-minute drive, very few words were spoken. When they arrived home, Randy and Dave lingered outside while Randy's mother and Rita went into the kitchen to talk. He just knew they didn't want the kids around.

Randy could hear the pair talking in the kitchen, so he told Dave to wait there in the driveway. Then he walked over to the kitchen window, where he could listen without being seen.

"The next thing I remember hearing was them talking to one another and saying, 'Well, what did *you* see?' My mother said that she looked around, and she peered in one of the side windows. What she saw was a gaunt, elderly man holding one of the older-style phones, with the ear-piece up to his ear, standing frozen in this death grimace. And between his lower arm and upper arm, where it was bent holding the phone she actually saw cobwebs. That image was horrifying to me. There was something about it that stuck in my head.

"Then Rita said she'd gone around the other side of the building, and she had seen an elderly man dressed in overalls staring out of one of the windows. Covered in dust. My mother did mention the people were dressed in clothes of the '30s or '40s. From what I overheard, there was no reaction to anyone looking at them. There was just a dead-on, unblinking stare. Their eyes were like saucers. Wide open and staring out.

"They were terrified by what they saw," Randy said of his mother and her friend. "The reaction was immediate, and it was 'this is not right.' There was no question in their minds that these guys weren't dead, but they weren't alive. How can I put it? If there was ever a limbo, it was what they saw and how they described it."

Randy is unclear as to how much time passed before his father heard the story and wanted to see the house for himself. "It could have been a week, a month, but it was no more than two or three months later." Randy cleared his throat and continued. "I was with them when they decided to go back. I think it was more or less against my mother's wishes." Randy's recollection was that he was a little nervous about going back but didn't really expect to see anything. His mother and Rita, however, were in the back seat, terrified that they were even going near that house again. "My mother was hesitantly giving directions to my dad," said Randy. "I remember knowing that road was definitely the road we were on. There were a lot of shrubs and trees surrounding the area where this house was. But when we got to the clearing, there was no house. There was nothing there. My mother was shocked. I don't know what my dad thought. There wasn't a foundation there, like the house had been demolished. And this was the spot. There's not that much area there. We had lived on the Cape for years, so we knew our way around. It was not there. It was like it never existed."

The experience left a permanent impression on Randy, who has an interest in the offbeat and unusual. "From that moment on, I would tell my friends that they were the 'Freeze Men,'" he said of the wide-eyed, staring people whose description frightened him so much as a kid, "because they were frozen in time. I would try to scare them with warnings to watch out for the 'Freeze Men!' Until I got older. Then it became sort of ridiculous in a bizarre way."

Because his mother never knew he heard what she saw, Randy never felt comfortable enough to bring up the subject with her. He never even told Dave what he heard. But as the years went by, every now and then he would think about the incident again. "And the details were always clear in my head—the ones that I remember."

As for the experience itself, Randy said, "I can't explain it. If you can't put that in some kind of rational context, what can you say about it?" The best analogy he can come up with is to a snapshot. "What if you walked into an old picture and walked out? Not to sound dramatic, but we found this place, and these people out of time, for a moment. We saw this snapshot out of time."

BETWEEN A ROCK AND
A HARD PLACE

*When we stopped by Taryn Thoman's shop on Main Street in
Hyannis, we brought records from the Registry of Historic
Deeds about her former home on Kalmus Beach. Over the
phone, Taryn had expressed interest in the history of the
house. At a desk in the back of the store, with an old-fashioned
cash register in front of boxes of minerals, she carefully stud-
ied the names of the previous owners and the years they
owned the house. Taryn felt that the house she had rented for
five winters was actually a back house to a main house that
was wiped out in a storm. A former professional guitarist,
Taryn has expressive green eyes and long blond hair. On display in her store were sterling silver and gold jewelry, stones
and minerals (including some gemstones believed to have
metaphysical properties), fossils, milkweed seed light catchers,
and other rare, visually-pleasing merchandise.*

W hen I first was looking at places to rent for the
winter, a real estate agent took me to the home on
Kalmus Beach. I didn't even need to go in the house. We

just pulled in the driveway and I said, "I'll take it." I loved the house. I really thought at some point I would be able to afford to buy it. But the owner was asking five hundred thousand dollars. I couldn't get near that price range. I just kept living there and scrambling for places to live in the summertime when the rent went way up.

I moved in and out of the house five times. So I had tons of stuff that I had stuck up in the attic. It was a typical attic with a bulb socket in the front end and another in the back. It was laid out so that if somebody went up there and redid the whole thing, they could have a two-room loft. It was a decent pad up there. For whatever reason, though, it was very cool in the right part of the attic. And it was on the right side that stuff always happened. I would put my stuff there, and I would come up in the spring, or whenever, and it would be moved to the other side. Like somebody went up, picked it up, and moved it. I was the only one living there. I was the only one who went up there. I knew I had locked the door and nobody else had access. I simply stayed away from the attic most of the time. So I didn't really confirm the situation very often.

What's interesting is that so many people have these experiences, and yet it's not something that is accepted. I find that so amazing. I know the cat didn't want to go up there, and the cat goes everywhere. He went up there once and went around the corner. All his hair stood up on end, and he turned around and ran downstairs. I just had a certain understanding with whatever was there in the attic, like, "I'm just here to put my stuff here and I'm out!"

She laughs.

The house was right on the water. It was often loud. I

would think I'd hear noises when I first moved there, and I got very frightened a lot—I lived there by myself. It's one huge, big house right on the water, and the wind just smashed against it. So you could let your imagination pretty much tell you anything. During big storms I loved to sit on the bed because the house would just rock and make all kinds of noises. I heard stuff moving, but it could have been the storm and not anything in the attic. But lights often would go on and off in the house, and there would be other strange stuff. Like I said, I just accepted it. That's what it was. It wasn't there to hurt me.

Others who I had asked not to go in the attic did go in there. And they had weirder experiences than I did. I spent some time in Arizona, and the guy who was house-sitting called me and said there was something in the attic. He heard some noises, and he traced them to the attic. I said, "Look, just stay out of the attic." Instead, he called his friends to come over and they proceeded to drag a Ouija board up there. Friday night on Cape Cod. Nothing to do. Bring out the Ouija board and see what comes up. And that's just an invitation as far as I'm concerned. Come on in. Mess with my head. And that's exactly what happened.

As various things happened to them over the next several days, they went totally ballistic. Some of them aren't very comfortable talking about it even now. They heard voices over a period of several nights. Stuff got moved around. One of them left the Ouija board on the table, and when they came back it was leaning against the door of the attic. The guy who was actually staying at the house heard a wailing baby. It sounded like it came from a chair in the room. But there was no one in the chair. His friend heard evil voices following him down the road.

I think that you probably should be genuinely afraid of some of that stuff. The stuff that I've encountered, I don't have a great fear of, because it's not terribly threatening. I was trying to have a really simple spiritual life. I knew there was something going on. I knew there was something inhabiting that room. I just knew that internally. I have a perfect acceptance of whatever is there, and I don't need to go hunting it down or explaining it or anything. I didn't have a problem with it. I didn't go up and hang out in the attic and light candles, or have séances and invite ghost busters and people who go and have a look. It wasn't a big deal to me because I didn't make it one. It's there. I accept it, and I'm not going to fool with it. I never saw lamps flying across the room. I rely on my own spirituality and my own personal knowledge. If I were to feel threatened by something, then I would get out instead of going in the attic and prompting something to happen.

THREE-BEDROOM
COLONIAL WITH GHOST

*Bob Houst got into real estate because he enjoyed dealing
with people and knew something about land and property.
He felt his experience in running a guesthouse with his
family when he was young had given him an edge in relat-
ing to people. He described himself as a natural salesman
and scorned those in suits who graduated with business
degrees yet were clueless when it came to having rapport
with customers. A genial man with a ready smile, Bob wore
a plaid short-sleeved shirt and green sweatpants with no
socks. Occasionally he would interrupt his account to keep
tabs on a pit bull puppy named Serena, calling its name
while walking around after it. Bob sat at a large plastic
table in the backyard of his home on Main Street in West
Dennis, the deep blue Bass River visible in the distance.*

Serena! Serena! Get down! I'm so embarrassed. She's a pit
bull. They want to chew, they want to bite. I just thought
it was such a nice day and she would just sit out here.

Well, I know of a few haunted houses. I've lived here thirty-three years. I'm a realtor, and knew there was a "presence" in a house I sold five years ago. The seller and I felt this very strongly. We told the buyers, and we put in the contract, "The premises have been known to contain 'ghosts.'" It sounds silly, but now I understand that's an issue in real estate that people should disclose. Now, the buyers didn't take it seriously. They rehabbed the house. They did a beautiful job. It's a bed and breakfast now, and Olympic skaters have been renting it for the past three or four summers. They put them up there. It's very nice. They did a nice job.

I was once selling a house on Fiske Street. Since I was a kid, in that whole area, there have always been sightings of people in white dresses. The house I was selling had been in the owner's family forever. She took me downstairs, and I saw it had a beehive oven and a low ceiling. She said in the cold weather they used to live down in this kind of kitchen-living room area. Because it had the big beehive oven it was warm, and it was out of the wind. I hadn't been downstairs more than two seconds when I saw a quick image of a man with a black suit and one of those top hats that they used to wear. He looked like Abe Lincoln, just standing there. I blinked, and it was gone. It's hard to say if that was my imagination.

But my main experience in the house was more obvious. A friend of mine, a young man in his twenties, had just gotten married, and he was considering buying the place with his in-laws so I took him to see it. We went through the house. We got up to the attic, which is kind of a scary, haunted attic, with eaves and beams. There were ropes hanging. And we were laughing about it. It just seemed strange up there. As we were talking, we started hearing this loud rapping. Very loud. It almost sounded like somebody had a club or a baseball bat and was banging very loudly and steadily. It was almost deafening. We went downstairs to try to find it. We went to the first floor, then we went down to the basement. And as we moved, it sounded like the noise moved. When we were upstairs, it sounded like it was coming from downstairs. And when we were downstairs, it sounded like it was coming from upstairs. And this continued for fifteen minutes. Finally, we thought, "This is really creepy." We went out into the driveway near the barn, and we could still hear it.

So I called the owner of the house, and, when I explained what happened, she said, "Oh, that must have been my great-grandfather." She said that he used to rap his cane when he was mad about something. She said that something about my friend must have upset him greatly. She later showed me pictures of him, and it looked like the man that I had seen in the basement, with this kind of black hat and cape.

I went back there several times later. There was never anything else. I had been there fifty times before that, and there was never really anything. But that one experience was so vivid and loud. My first reaction had been that somebody was in the house, teasing us. I really didn't think it was a spirit. I honestly felt there were some teenagers with a baseball bat or something. We were both just scratching our heads, amazed at how loud it was. My friend said, "I don't think I want this house." And we left.

There's a house on Route 6A called the Thacher House. It's owned by the Society for the Preservation of New England Antiquities. When I grew up, a family by the name of White lived there. And everybody was always seeing ghosts. Especially the children. It had a lot of period furniture and the big beds and you'd wake up and there'd be two or three little children spirits at the foot of the bed. I bet there are at least a hundred people who will tell stories about the Thacher house. During the time the Whites lived there, it was kind of a hangout.

I've had guests tell me that they've seen what they thought were ghosts right here in my home. There were a brother and sister who were visiting the Cape from Upstate New York. Each had an experience of someone standing in the room—standing over them or touching them. They were kind of nervous and went back to sleep. They didn't tell each other. And then, on the way home, when they were all the way to Connecticut, near the New York border, they called me back to ask if this was a common occurrence.

A few years earlier, some young women had made a similar claim. They were staying up in that same room. They were around twenty-two years old, and they were loaded—a lot of these kids go out here to the bars and they drink—so I didn't really take them that seriously. But this brother and sister went whale watching, and they were eating nuts and berries for breakfast. They didn't strike me as the type that would be under the influence. So that's two cases of it. There must be a lot of ghosts in West Dennis. I think they move around in these old captains' houses.

I've heard millions of stories over the years. It's, you know, the case history of the Cape. It seems like all the colorful people—the drinkers, the smokers, the wicked ones—all seemed to come down here to escape the Puritans in Boston. It's always been kind of a wild place. You know, you talk about P-town as the hell town and all that. I think the whole Cape has a flavor of that energy that carries on. When the most uncreative, mundane, middle class accountants come here, they can go crazy. And that's a common thing that happens on these soft, summer nights. It could be the salt air, or I think it's a supernatural phenomenon. The ghosts have something to do with this behavior. There's just something here. It's a different energy.

SEEING IS BELIEVING

Those who know Jack Braginton-Smith as an author and bibliophile appreciate his vast knowledge of history and his insatiable curiosity. But the seventy-four-year-old restaurateur is also locally famous for his homespun hospitality. Hidden behind shops along Route 6A in Yarmouth Port, Jack's Outback is a local meeting spot and an affordable place for down-home American cooking.

After enjoying a sign outside his front door that reads, "If there's a big line, use your brane; Go Away!" we stepped into the cafeteria-style restaurant and took in the handwritten menu, tacked to the wall and brimming with intentional misspellings. Jack, who was drying a spaghetti pot behind the counter, greeted us with a warm gaze and told us he had stopped serving lunch. We reintroduced ourselves and reminded him that he had agreed to meet with us that day. Putting his hand gently to his face, he muttered a mild expletive as he remembered the appointment. He asked us to take a seat in one of the booths in the rear of the restaurant.

*The dining area was empty. All that could be heard was
the clash of mounds of silverware as Jack's employees
worked busily to clean the kitchen. A ceiling fan spun quietly overhead.*

*After a brief conversation with a sales representative,
Jack joined us in the booth. He peered at us curiously with
an earnest expression. A few wisps of gray hair stood up
from his head. As he spoke, his wavering voice and deadpan
sense of humor made it impossible for us to decide whether
he had really forgotten who we were for a moment or had
only been having some fun.*

I had an incident on Route 6A at the Old Crocker
Tavern, which is now an inn. It scared the hell out of me.
I was living upstairs at the tavern. I had an enormous
room. I was up watching the telly at nine or ten at night in
one of the bedrooms. I was just in my shorts. And I heard
somebody coming up the stairs. I said, "Jesus Christ!
Nobody should be coming in the building. The doors are
locked." There was no way that could have been a tree
branch blowing against the house or a blind hitting the
windowsill. You could hear definite footsteps coming up
the stairs. So I hopped off the bed. The landing at the top
of the stairs was right outside my bedroom. I went over
and opened the door. Just as I opened it, I said to myself,
"Idiot! You're standing here in your shorts. If someone has
broken in and they're coming upstairs, what the hell are
you gonna do?" By then it was too late. I had opened the
door. And nothing was there. There was no place anyone
could have gone. The landing came up and there were my
door and two other doors, but they were both shut. It was

too short a period of time for the person to have gotten to a door from the landing—even if they ran like hell. So that scared the hell out of me. That was a good show.

I wasn't there much longer, but I certainly never felt much at ease when I was awake at night. I was always on the defensive. My ear was listening to the television, but there was always, "What was that?" The other thing I felt in the house was cold spots. But I think that was fear.

The older I get, the further away I get from believing something happened then. I know it happened, but my subconscious says it's not logical. Then again, in 1989 I had another funny thing happen. I was living in a friend's house in Cotuit for six months. I was sitting with my housemates in a big living room. There was a symphony playing on the turntable with a spindle. And about halfway through, the music stopped, the needle went back, and the record lifted off the turntable. Then it dropped back again. I mean, we all saw it. There was no explanation for what caused it—not a heavy truck driving by or a pet that could have knocked it.

There were a great many things of that nature that went on in that house. One morning I was sitting alone at the kitchen table having some cereal. And somebody patted me on the hiney. It was a brush-by pat. I thought it was a cat. I turned around, but the cat wasn't in the room. There was no one there. But somebody just brushed me. And that made a believer out of me because it wasn't a muscle twitch. When somebody touches you, you know you've been touched. While I was living there, my son Brian came to visit me from Yarmouth, and I think he had been playing sports. He went to take a shower, and he was soaping up when somebody patted him on the fanny. He came downstairs and said, "Jesus Christ. I was taking a shower up there and somebody patted me on the ass!"

I never felt scared there. Some houses you go into, they're cold and they're kind of ominous. You have an uneasy sense when you go into the house. And some houses are very warm, friendly, and protective. Rick Jones has a house that was built in 1678 just down the road in Cummaquid. When you go into that house you feel protected, warm, and confident.

I used to get that sensation walking along Route 6A to work—a little over a mile. At five-thirty in the morning, there's not much traffic. I'd see candles in the windows of these old houses, and I used to sense that independence and spirit of what Cape Cod used to be.

The Crocker Tavern had a lot of Cape Cod history to it because taverns were so extremely important back in the eighteenth century. They were the fulcrum of social and business activity in every community in New England that was close to the water. The tavern keepers were judges and justices of the peace, and the taverns had many things going on. They would sell shiploads of this and that, contracts, and insurance. It was a viable commercial entity. The Crocker Tavern has a lot of Barnstable history. The stairs at that tavern were worn all the way up, where for over two hundred years people had been walking up and down. The stairs had beautiful woodwork. What great steps!

LOST AND FOUND

Moved from a plot of land right behind the Dennis Public Market, Pat Short's home is located on a quiet side street off the well-traveled main roads to the Dennis Town Landing. With its dormers and one-car garage, at first glance the former Dennis Post Office blends right in with the neighboring houses that were built after the Second World War. But on closer inspection, the charm of an eighteenth-century three-quarter Cape shows through. One takes note of the antique narrow-paned windows that look like smiling eyes and the roofline that, like a furrowed brow, hugs the window tops.

With an addition in the back, the home is also deceptively large. Pat's living room is spacious and open with sunlight streaming in and a sliding back door leading out to an in-ground swimming pool. The interior of the home seems to mirror the quiet friendliness of the Short family. Wrapping her legs with her arms, Pat spoke with unassuming honesty of her family's diverse experiences in the home.

My mother was sleeping in the guest bedroom upstairs back in 1976, when she woke up at about four o'clock in the morning to find somebody about thirty-five years old lying in the bed next to her laid out like at a funeral. He had on what looked like a minister's garb. The long black coat, the white shirt, the little black thing at the neck, and lots and lots of jet-black hair and very sharp features. He looked like he had been sick for quite a while. He was so real looking, she felt if she put her hand on him, she could have touched him. She looked away and said, "I'm going to turn the light on, and you'll be gone." So she turned the light on, looked back, and he was gone. She still wishes she had asked him why he was there. He was so real, it wasn't as though you could look through him or anything.

What my mother didn't know is that Reverend Caleb Holmes, the first owner of the house, died when he was thirty-five years old. Back then the house sat across the street from a cemetery. So the chance of him being laid out for his funeral in that room was probably excellent.

That bedroom has had a lot of strange happenings. When we first found the house, back before we moved it, I was sitting in that room meditating, and I felt a cat climb into my lap and curl up and go to sleep. We didn't have a cat. When I opened my eyes, there was nothing in my lap. So that was awfully strange. We did find a dead cat in the attic under the eaves.

The house was going to be torn down, so we had to move it when we bought it. And when we moved it, I really felt that any spirits would stay in the old plot where the house had been. I didn't expect them to follow the house. But they did.

I've had some guests who've slept in the room and they've been fine. I've had others who've slept there and found it very unnerving. My oldest son lives in Hyannis now. But he used to have parties at the house, and he'd show his buddies the room where the ghost slept. Then he would bang on the wall and the kids would scream "Aaaah!" and go running out.

When Robin, a friend of mine, went into the front part of the house at night, she'd feel like something was following her. She'd turn around and see it, then see it disappear. So nobody really wanted to sleep in the front of the house.

Doors opening and shutting by themselves is almost a given around here. Even if the door is latched, the door will just open up. My daughter, Becky, who is now a senior in high school, has grown up with it and doesn't consider it that bizarre or unusual to have doors opening and shutting. When she was little, she slept in the back part. When she was ten or eleven, she had a really bad night. Whatever it was kept opening the door. It just would not stop. So she latched the door, and she said to it, "If you open this door one more time, I'm not sleeping in this room." Much to her amazement, the door opened up again. I went to wake her in the morning and found out she had climbed into the bathtub with her pillow and blankets and had slept in there that night. But she eventually just got used to it. After a while, she decided even if it opened and shut the door, she was just going to ignore it. Sometimes she'd feel its presence. But she never let it bother her after that.

Becky, who entered the room minutes earlier, laughs and casually adds, "There was also this guy dressed all in brown who had a little hat and cane, and he used to stand at the foot of my bed and say 'Good night' and then 'Sweet dreams,' and he would go away. The first couple of times this happened, I got really scared. But then I thought, 'Oh, he's here again and he's saying good night and everything.' It was weird. It was really odd. He was a very common, pleasant, gentle guy. But rather odd events happen when you're twelve years old, and you think, 'What's going on?' I would also definitely hear voices sometimes downstairs when everybody else was asleep. Just people talking and shouting and laughing, and as I tried to ignore it and rationalize it as the wind, the door latch was lifting and the doors would open and close. That's when I slept in the tub. Mom, tell about all the items that appear and disappear. I lost my birthday cards once. They had all been sitting there with my money and stuff in them. I was really mad. Then they showed up on the dining room table two weeks later. The money was still in there. Lots of our stuff disappears."

Well, funny things like that happen in this old house, and I'm sure in many others. Pearl earrings disappear and reappear. I'm always cleaning and vacuuming every inch of this house. Then I often go into the dining room and find a slip of paper on the floor from something I bought fifteen years ago. And I have no idea where that came from. I've found stuff on the dining room table, and I've always asked, "Who put this here?" Nobody saw it and nobody put it there. Yet it just appeared. I've lost jewelry. Sometimes I've said,

"Okay, I'm just going to let it go. I'm not going to hunt for it." And it will just reappear. Sometimes it will reappear on the dining room table. I have no explanation for how it gets there, what happened, or anything. The kids have had similar experiences. The strange thing I don't understand is those old slips that just turn up out of nowhere. You find one on the table and throw it out, then there's a second one. And how in Heaven's name? You just went through and cleaned the entire house, and there's the slip for seventy-nine cents dated July 6, 1983. I no doubt would have thrown that receipt away as soon as I got it.

The dining room has always been a busy room. Sometimes, when you're in the house, you'll see someone out of the corner of your eye. Then you'll go to focus on him, and he's already gone. For some reason, the dining room also stays extra cool. Even in the hottest days of summer, the coolest room will always be the dining room. And it faces south.

My brother slept in the guestroom. Because my mother had had the experience before my brother slept there, I once asked him, "Are you disturbed by anything at night? Because Momma had her ghost in there." "No," he said, "it doesn't bother me. But those people partying in the dining room every night are driving me crazy. If they would just stop moving the chairs around, I'd be fine."

I don't know what woke me up one night, but you know how you just have an intuitive feeling? It was shortly after we had moved in. I had been doing restoration on the house. We tore down the ceiling—of course, right after I'd oiled all my furniture. We were burning up a lot of the stuff we were throwing out. One night I woke up, and it was almost like something was standing at the foot of the bed. But it wasn't a scary feeling. It was like somebody was trying to get me to wake up because something wasn't right. When I fully opened my eyes, it was gone. But I felt uneasy so I got up to check on the house anyway. As I got to the top of the stairs and I looked down, I saw paper in the fireplace starting to ignite and rolling off of the hearth onto the wooden floor. So I came racing downstairs and got the paper back in, and I thought, "If whatever it was hadn't awakened me, the house could have caught fire and burned down." That gives me goose bumps just to think about it even now.

I had the house blessed, and I told the priest to bless the guestroom especially, and I started telling the ghost story. I guess I shouldn't have done that. He bolted. He blessed it really fast. You never saw holy water go so fast in your life. And that priest went out the door so fast. I had made coffee and coffee cake, and I thought I'd give him that. Usually you give them a gratuity or something. But no chance. Just, Poom! "Thank you, Pat! Bye!"

I always thought it would be nice to not worry and live in a place where this kind of thing doesn't happen. Still, when I come down at night and go to turn on the light switch, my hand goes around hoping nothing is gonna— "oooh"—go over me. But I don't worry about it as much anymore because, even though we've had ghosts, nothing malevolent has ever happened. In fact, after the fire in the dining room that night, I felt whatever presence is here is a good presence. It seems to like us.

HOME

Our conversation took place in the Mashpee Public Schools Indian Education office, a classroom decorated with children's murals and poems at Kenneth C. Coombs Elementary School. Joan Tavares-Avant was sitting behind a teacher's desk, talking on the phone, her salt and pepper hair bundled, her glasses forward. In the middle of the room, a young woman with long black hair sat at two school desks pulled together, sorting through laminated newspaper articles. She confidently looked over at us, smiling. Joan hung up and instructed us to pull loose chairs up to her desk. As we explained our project, she nodded attentively. Then, in a soft, pensive voice, she began saying what happens at her house and how she, as a Wampanoag tribal member, perceives it. As she spoke, she rolled forward and backward in her swivel chair, her stare locking on one of us and then on the other as she conveyed ideas that challenge traditional assumptions about haunted houses.

Well, I live in a house that belongs to my family. Some people call it "haunted," and some of them are afraid to come by because of the stories they've heard— the oral stories they've heard from the tribal members.

She sits up straight and places her arms on her desk.

I look at it as just the opposite. As a Wampanoag tribal member, I understand that the sounds you hear or the things you may see come from my ancestors, who are protecting us and guiding us.

When you say "haunted," people have a tendency to say it's eerie, it's scary—it gives it a different connotation.

I believe that life and death are one, like the earth and the sky, the river and the seas. That type of association. I don't believe that there's a real end. That's my sense because ever since I was very young, I've held connections with people—a relative or someone in the community— even after their death. I feel that person is my guide, also my protector, my support mechanism. He or she gives me no fear whatsoever.

So, I could never use the word "haunt" in terms of it being a haunted house. I would say that it's a home with ancestral spirits.

Let me give an example in terms of my being here as Indian education director. My grandmother has passed on, but she still continues to provide strength for me to do what I'm doing for the next generation. She did it for generations before me, and she is doing it for my generation. And I just happen to be the one to grasp that. Even late at night I feel her presence, her guiding me to carry on the Wampanoag traditions as she did. I think that's wonderful.

Winnie is listening.

The young woman in the middle of the room laughs knowingly.

Do you feel that way sometimes, Winnie?

"Mmm-hmm," says Winnie, nodding.

She's a tribal member, also. She's younger than I am, but we both have a very strong feeling that when our relatives leave us, they haven't gone. Winnie, I don't know if you've heard stories over at my house or not. . .

Winnie nods.

. . .but in my home, you could be sitting just like you and I are sitting right now, and maybe a cabinet door might just come ajar. Okay, that's happened hundreds of times in my home. You may be sitting like this and that shade might just go pshhhh! You may be sitting and eating and you could feel that someone is walking past you. Someone is right there, and I just feel it.

And there's no reason to be afraid. I don't believe there's any reason to be afraid. The ones to be afraid of are the people who are alive, not the ones that are trying to protect you.

My uncle told a lot of stories about my home when he was younger. And my mother has told various stories. And they've been similar. They've had similar experiences— like hearing footsteps or hearing somebody move around upstairs, and there's nobody up there. Or like going to the sink and seeing a pot of water and no one has any memory of putting water in the pot.

Sometimes in the middle of the night I hear the pipes dancing. I call it dancing or drumming—but it is coming through the pipes. Those sounds are evident. Sometimes, I actually wait for the sounds. I find them very comforting. Some community people say, "Well, why don't you go to church on Sunday?" or something like that. My home, that's what's church to me. That's what I'm comfortable with.

My house is old and crooked and whatever you want to call it. But I've had people go there and say, "Oh, this feels like home." I'm even talking about strangers. Because I'm a very community-oriented person I come in contact with a lot of people. They come in and say how comfortable they are. And sometimes I kind of raise my eyebrows, too. But they wouldn't have any need to mention that so there has got to be some truth to their comments.

My family has lived in that house since it was built, and that has been well over 150 years. We've always had a connection with our ancestors, relatives, and community people. It feels like they're knocking at your door. They're coming, and they're coming with a purpose.

Oftentimes you may not be able to make that connection, but down the road it may come to you and you'll say, "Oh, I remember that happening." Maybe the shade went up and it went up roughly. In the next few days, something may happen. It might be something nice, might be something bad. But there are always signs.

I don't know whether you can understand what I'm saying. It's a feeling. It's hard for me to define. It's hard to say just what it is, unless you can catch me at a time when it has just happened.

"It's hard when nobody knows what you're experiencing. You can't really explain it," says Winnie.

It's not supernatural or anything like that.

"And it's not something that everybody feels, either. Not everybody gets that spiritual experience."

In my mind, it just happens. Did you ever sit in a chair and have the chair start to move? That happens sometimes to me. It probably is not time for you to sit down, but to keep on moving.

Sitting in that house, I will be watching TV or something, and I'll see something move. And it's always out of the corner of my eye. I've never figured it out, but it's always out of the corner of it. Not if I turn my head. I've woken up at night sometimes and seen my own people. I see them near a nightstand or near a bureau. This is when they talk to me. You know, for as long as I live—or live as you see me—I'll always be a receiver for my ancestors. I'll always be receiving something, and it's generally something that's positive, trying to direct me to do something that's of need. Or trying to tell me something is going to happen and I'm going to need to help with it. If I can't make a connection sometimes when that happens, later on—it might be six months down the road—I can link it.

Sometimes I lie across the bed at night with the blankets

propped up, and I like to put my feet under them. Last night around five o'clock, something was quivering under my feet. And nobody was there.

I don't know what meaning it has. I haven't connected that yet. But that's one of the things that has happened.

The phone rings and Joan picks up immediately. She pushes back her chair and begins talking. Winnie holds up one of the articles she is laminating and says it is about her uncle, David Hendricks, who was shot and killed by a police officer.

"We still do a memorial walk the date he got shot to keep his spirit around," she says, "and then we have a little ceremony and go back to the house for a potluck supper. There are five hundred people just on the walk, just to keep that spirit alive so that he'll never be gone.

"My uncle was the Dragonfly, and it's so weird—one time, I was just sitting in a chair outside sunning, and he flew right on me when I was just sitting there. And though usually I'm scared of bugs, he just kept crawling on me."

Joan hangs up the phone and rejoins the conversation.

What, Winnie?

"You know how my Uncle David is the Dragonfly?"

Yeah.

"Well, one day I was just sunning outside. He just crawled up. After a while he just flew away. The next day I went to

sit in that chair, but he was already sitting there. Everyone has their stories."

I have many stories about my beliefs and experiences.

"I think you have to have that belief in you. You can't just think, 'Oh, when is it going to happen to me?' Things like that don't just happen. You have to have that belief inside of you."

Believe me, when you tell me I'm dead and you put me in a casket, I ain't going too far.

Believe that to the day you die. I intend to be around. I'm going to guide my people. And I might be stronger than my own ancestors are in my house—in a positive sense. If I don't have enough time on this earth to guide my people, there's more time.

I've got grandchildren, and I've got next generations to come who I'm going to be guiding with the teachings of my ancestors from when they were alive and after they crossed over.

Today I still have some of the stories my grandmother used to tell about things that go on in the Tribe. Just talking about history in general. Her talking about her mother and her father and what they did, their way of life, and so forth gives you a lot of strength. It's like my uncle Peter who drank. He was really an alcoholic. I don't look at him as an alcoholic. I look at him as a man who really gave me strength. He gave up a lot of good times to tell us a lot of good stories. A lot of good legends. I think it pulled something positive out of that man that still fills my life. I don't concentrate on the social ills that he had. I just choose not to. I don't grab at negativity.

I have an association with nursing homes. And in these nursing homes I find people who have relatives who have just thrown them in there and forgotten about them. I just think that's the saddest thing in the world. My uncle was the hardest man in the whole wide world to take care of. He died of cancer. But I struggled and struggled to keep him. I know some people just have to let go because their relatives need nursing care. But, because I have strong beliefs, I just had to hold onto him and just take care of him in my home, and he died in my arms. Maybe I'm sort of opinionated in some ways. But I have very strong family beliefs, tribal beliefs also. I really do.

DISCOVERY

"You must be the ghost guys," said Chrystal LaPine, letting us in through a side door facing her driveway. She drank from a glass of water at the kitchen sink. "I just got up not long ago. I was working until four in the morning because of the fire in Hyannis."

She had short blond hair, warm green eyes, and a casual, assured aura that made our discussion feel like ordinary conversation.

A dispatcher in the sheriff's office for Barnstable County, she was formerly a police officer for the town of Sandwich. She responded to a burglar alarm at the Dillingham House on Main Street in Sandwich late one night in February of 1983 and subsequently fled in a hurry.

"It opened me to some thoughts that I didn't ever consider as being factual," she said, in a breathless, flowery voice. "Being in the house—it was almost like having your mind opened to the fact that something genuinely does happen when somebody passes away. It's very hard to explain. But it was eye-opening."

Her two-year-old son, Ben, was asleep in a room off the kitchen. She led us to the kitchen table and sat down, crossing her legs—quiet, relaxed, seemingly waiting for a question. We asked her if, as a police officer, she ever regretted going public with this kind of story.

Well, I kept it to myself for years. The only ones I discussed it with were the other officer, Jim, who was there, and my husband. The only reason my involvement came out was because Jim did an article in the little town newspaper and mentioned my name; then they came to me for substantiation. I had not told anybody because it had previously happened to Jim. I remember how everybody razzed him when he told people. We all gave him such a hard time that he never opened his mouth again. So I wasn't about to say anything. But I saw nothing outrageous like people flying through the room or anything. It was just all very strange things that happened that can't be explained. At least they've never been explained to me in any satisfactory way. I'm really thick-skinned. In this line of work, I think you have to be.

The first time I ever went to the Dillingham House was for a day alarm. I went with another officer. The building was shut up for the winter. We just walked through the house; looked here, there, and everywhere; secured doors; and left. It was no big deal.

It's a real antique home. The cellar was one of those old-fashioned Cape cellars. Have you been in the house? Wow, it's really wild! It's gorgeous! The cellar is all stone with round walls. Evidently, they ran slaves through the cellar, as part of the Underground Railroad. It's an intriguing house, because it's got all different kinds of secret places, like behind the closet upstairs: when you open the closet, you can pull the shelves down and a stairway folds out that goes up into a hidden attic.

It still has the footed tubs and the old, wide shiplap pine floors and stuff. It always intrigued me because it was such an old house. Just a really nice house. Beautiful.

But that was the initial alarm, and we got a follow-up call late one night at about two in the morning that somebody reported seeing lights on in the house. But when I pulled up there in the driveway, there were no lights. It was just an alarm.

I got out of my cruiser and went up to the side door, and the door was locked. Then I remembered that I didn't have my flashlight. As I said, there were no lights on. So I went back to my cruiser and got my flashlight, and I turned around and the lights were on upstairs and the side door was open. I said, "Hmmm, I was just there. I don't remember that door being open." So I sprung in the door. It's hard to explain to civilians, but as a police officer you're mainly concerned with your own safety. I went around with a flashlight. I walked through the kitchen and into the living room. Then I heard a click and a hum. "What the heck is that?" Then I was back in the kitchen and the microwave oven was on. I was looking at it, and I said, "That's ridiculous. The microwave came on all by itself. Okay, it must be something electrical. That's why the alarm went off. Something shorted in the house." I didn't give it a second thought. I just kept on going. I walked through the living room. The room was beautiful. There was a rocking chair in one corner. All lace curtains on all the windows. It was sparsely furnished, like the old days, but it was very nice. I thought I heard somebody walking around upstairs. I distinctly heard footsteps. So I went upstairs, checked all the bedrooms, and checked everything up there. I checked the closet and behind doors. That's how I found the closet with the shelves that lead up to the hidden attic. There was nothing up there. There wasn't anyone anywhere. Then I heard doors slam, so I knew the other cruiser was there, and I talked to the officer over the portable and I had him check the perimeter of the house. And he reported that he didn't see anything on the outside.

I had checked all the doors. I checked everything up there, and there was nothing. Then I was remembering all the stories that Jim had told me about the night he'd been in there and something had happened to him, and I thought, "Hmmm!" But I didn't really believe it was that. Then I heard somebody walking around downstairs. I thought the other officer had come in the house, so I went downstairs expecting to see him. And the rocking chair was rocking all by itself. It sounds so weird telling people this stuff. The rocking chair was rocking in the corner of the living room, and the lace curtains were blowing open like it was a summer day, but it was mid-winter. And there was no heat on in the house, because it was unoccupied. There were no heat registers to make the heat come up and blow the curtains. There were no windows open. It was dead of winter. I have no explanations. The rocking chair was rocking away, and the curtains were all blowing. It got very eerie inside the house. It's hard to explain. When I was in the middle of the house—even though I'm a cop and have a gun and everything else—and all these things were starting to happen around me that I couldn't explain, I was thinking, "Well, I'm out of here." I went out front, and, just as I was going out, the other guy was coming in. He looked around the corner, saw the rocker and the curtains, and he said, "See ya." And he left.

It was very minor, but there was no question something took place. It was very strange. On the other hand, it was fun. I didn't feel I was going to be hurt. I was scared because I couldn't figure out why these things were happening—it didn't scare me like anybody was going to come out of the closets and hack me to pieces.

I have never had an experience like that since then. It's weird, because when you're in my line of work, you're always exposed to people dying. I mean, I've sat in cars with people when they die. I've got into cars after accidents, and they've been alive and died while I was with them. And that never bothered me until this. And then I kept thinking, "Jeez, you know, what's happening inside this person? A minute ago this person was alive. But they didn't stand a chance and they passed away with me sitting next to them, trying to bring 'em back in a car." And it makes you wonder what happens. Ever since being in that house and seeing that maybe this kind of thing takes place, you have to actually consider what's happening to their soul while you're sitting there in the car. Being with somebody in that circumstance after being in the house was very strange for me. I remember one girl, specifically, because she was young. She was nineteen, and I just happened to be behind her when she drove off the road and hit a tree. And she died instantly. But I crawled inside the car to check her, and I can remember being overwhelmed by really strange feelings of wanting to get out of the car really fast. And that had never happened before.

You're taught in Sunday School and then in church that your soul lives on—you go to Heaven and everything else—but you never really think of it realistically because, let's face it, nobody ever thinks of passing away when they're young. When all of a sudden you're faced with the possibility that there is something afterwards, it opens your mind to a whole new realm of possibilities. You think these things are going to happen only to somebody who is paranormal, or somebody who is very out-there somewhere. Or somebody who does channels or tunes into things. But it's not true.

It's all just real, everyday kind of stuff.

When I came out of the house, the other officer knew something had happened by the look on my face. He looked at me, and he said, "You saw it, didn't you?" And he discussed it a bit, but not a lot, because you also have to realize you're dealing with the cop persona, too. Policemen have a very hard outer shell. They don't let a lot get in.

You can't. You'd be nuts if you did.

So you have to understand you're dealing with that kind of attitude. And, to be honest with you, I wouldn't be surprised if it happened to some of the others, and they will never, ever admit it in a hundred years.

Now I work in the Emergency Communication Center.

We do all the fire mutual aid for the whole Cape. I dispatch all the trucks and send all the mutual aid. We supervise all police dispatches for the whole Cape. We do rescues as far off as Marion, Mattapoisett, and Rochester, and then all the way to P-town. We do Coast Guard, civilian med flights from Boston, and stuff like that. It's so multifaceted, it never gets boring.

As a police officer, I responded to those calls. We did business and house alarms all the time. Mostly outside meter alarms that would go off from wind or lightning. Everybody's alarm goes in a thunderstorm.

But that night at the Dillingham House was a very calm night. It was very cold. We weren't having any storms. It wasn't windy. I've searched my brain high and low for a reason. I just know that it doesn't end when they put you in the ground. That's the only certainty that I've come away with.

A MATTER OF LIFE
AND DEATH

*On a gray February afternoon, Jerry Ellis, the caretaker and
superintendent, led us on a tour of the Sagamore Cemetery, a
private village graveyard on Route 6A in Bourne. A devoted
board member of the local historic commission and retired
Korean War Air Force crew member and pilot, Jerry took obvious pride in the eighty-two war veterans and twenty-five sea
captains who were among those resting in the small, quiet
cemetery. Walking deliberately from stone to stone, he pointed
out to us representatives of well-known Cape families, bearing
names including Howes, Nye, Crowell, Swift, Perkins, Sears,
Gibbs, Bearse, and Eldridge. Since his family has been living
in the area since 1632, many of his own relatives and forbears
are among them.*

*The locally famous Dexter rhododendrons brought in
from Heritage Plantation would not bloom until spring.
Still, there was a diversity of trees: pine, gum, copper beech,
and red maple. Jerry said the cemetery relies on charitable
donations for the upkeep of the grounds.*

His sense of responsibility for the cemetery came through strongly as he moved along, imparting interesting facts about the occupants of various graves—the town fathers, influential industrialists, military men, and memorable town "characters." On the way to what he promised would be the scariest part of the cemetery, he seemed to take sly, slightly perverse enjoyment in our response to his occasional grisly remarks about "cold storage," weepholes that serve as drainage for every casket, graves that collapse, and coffins that break open. He chuckled as he recalled coming to the graveyard as a kid, where as one of a group he would climb on top of a mausoleum and breathe into a hole to make "real weird sounds" that would send the other kids running.

Pausing before the resting place of Captain William Burgess, he said he grew aware of his first ghost problem because of his habitual thoroughness in checking all the gravestones.

One day I found the headstone here off its base and resting against that headstone behind it. I said, "That's funny." The stone had been lifted up. There were no pry marks. There was absolutely no way that a fulcrum had been used to force it up. It always leaves an impression, no matter where you do it. There wasn't even a footprint in the hole that it came out of. It's inevitable because of the weight factor that you've got to crush in the sides. I mean, you cannot move that. If humans did it, it would show signs of movement. Who could do that? I can't pick it up. I invite you to put your hand on that stone and feel how heavy it is.

I took a photograph of the hole, and its edges were very defined. You can't see where they were pried with a crowbar, moved, or lifted.

Over here, these stones that had always been facedown had been turned over and were lying faceup against the base. Again, there was no sign of any movement. I've never noticed stones moved like that. Ever. Ever!

I had the police down here. That's how upset I was. I said to the police sergeant, "I don't know if you're going to believe this; it may be for *X-Files* or something, but if you've got an officer in the vicinity, would you tell him to stop by, because I've got something down here in the cemetery I can't explain." The cop who showed up was a little bit taken aback by what was going on. We could not find any signs—beer cans, cigarette wrappers, that type of thing—left behind. Are you talking about high-school kids lifting it? It would take six, maybe. Whenever you move anything that heavy, you have to leave some trace. Especially if it had been sitting facedown, and now all of a sudden it's completely uprooted and moved. Now, I'm not saying a supernatural moved it, but I don't know what moved it. So we've chalked it up to an unknown.

Jerry stops again at a shadowed, secluded area of the cemetery dotted with weathered, lichen-covered stones.

This area, along this whole wall, is the most haunted part of the cemetery. I don't care who you talk to who has been in here at night—this is the place where they get the daylight scared out of them.

This whole section of graves has been dug up and moved

from one of two other cemeteries. These old stones are from the Collins Farm Cemetery. When they dug the canal, this was right in the middle. The rest are from the Ellis Cemetery. Emory Ellis was a character who held off the state and the dredgers and the diggers with a shotgun at the entrance and wouldn't let them move the cemetery because it was a family plot. Finally, he relented after certain amounts of money passed hands, and in 1909, here it came.

A number of times, I've noticed an incredibly pungent odor of cigar smoke. Now come to find out, Emory Ellis was a big smoker of cigars. Whether it's him, or who, or what, I can't tell you. It's just that a number of people who have worked up here have experienced that same sensation.

Jerry describes a former caretaker and coworker who had spent time on lightships and told wild sea stories that would stand your hair on end.

He encountered cigar smoke on many occasions. I remember a specific incident—I think I was fourteen—of him waiting for me when I got off the school bus, to bring me up here to ask me if I smelled it. I didn't smell it right away, but before I went home that night, I did. If you come here at night, be my guest. If I have to come up here, I tend to stay away from this area.

Now, there are other areas of the graveyard where you get the feeling someone's watching you. I'll be honest with you. You can come up here, and you can be the bravest bastard who walks and you're going to be scared. Now, I was in Korea and got shot at a lot. But if you're standing out here at night, that's scary. It's a psychological thing. It's the fear of the unknown. And you know there's nothing there, but you don't know!

He laughs, then adds that the day after the former caretaker first pointed out the cigar smoke to him, they were walking through the same section when one of the graves caved in and the elder caretaker fell in.

For a sixty-three-year-old man, I never saw anyone move so fast in my life. It scared the living hell out of me. He had gone right into the casket. The whole thing had collapsed. So between him and me, we had some serious movement!

Then he said to me, "I wonder if that's where I smell the cigar smoke." And it wasn't three days later that I smelled the smoke there. In my lifetime of working in here, I've experienced it maybe twelve times. It's very distinct. You cannot distinguish it as anything other than cigar smoke. It's not cigarette smoke, and I don't smoke, personally. So when you get that smell, it's there. I would go to court on it.

I have a strong Irish heritage on my father's side, and I have a very strong tendency to believe in ghosts. There are a lot of ghosts lying around.

WORLDS IN COLLISION

An anonymous Woods Hole scientist shared this account of a strange thing that happened to him a number of years ago in an old house on the grounds of the Quissett campus of the Woods Hole Oceanographic Institution (WHOI).

The articulate, soft-spoken gentleman had first heard stories about institution guards who had quit supposedly because of what they encountered in the house, as well as rumors of their dogs howling when they were in the building. But he gave little thought to these stories until one early summer morning.

In the mid-1970s, the United States Geological Survey (USGS) made arrangements with WHOI to lease the stately old Quissett campus estate house as office space because the USGS Quissett campus facility was growing rapidly in response to the Arab oil embargo. The scientist was a member of the Geological Survey and was one of the first people to occupy the great, brooding hilltop house since it had been abandoned years before by its wealthy former owners. His

upstairs office was complete with delft tile fireplaces and a
mahogany flush-box bathroom, and had a sweeping view of
Nantucket Sound.

This is the scientist's story as he relates it:

About six o'clock on a beautiful summer morning, I was working in my office. I was in the habit of going to work quite early. It was a spectacular Cape Cod morning— so fine that it was hard to concentrate on my work. Birds sang cheerily in the Quissett Woods, and Nantucket Sound loomed vast and colorful in the sunrise to the northeast. Because it was a little bit windy, I had my office door closed so that the cross-draft would not blow papers off of my desk.

As I tried to work, I became aware of someone walking, with a very heavy and deliberate tread, up the central hall stairway, which was down the hall from my closed door. I heard a steady series of ka-thump-ka-thump-ka-thump-ka-thumps. Whoever was there walked up the stairway and, finally, at the top of the steps started to go down the hall with a remarkably heavy progression of steps. I didn't know who that could be. I wasn't used to anybody else working at that early hour.

I got up from my desk, opened the door, and looked down the hall to where I felt the sounds were emanating from. There was no one there, but the sounds had stopped. I thought that perhaps whoever was there had been alarmed by my opening the door, so I walked down the hall and looked down the stairs. I didn't see anyone so I thought that somehow I must have missed the person. There was a possibility he'd gone in some other door or ducked into a room or something, or that he had somehow left the building without me seeing him.

At this point I gave the event little further thought, went back to my office, closed the door, and tried to get back to work. Very shortly thereafter, the same heavy tread on the stairs began again. The insistent, deliberate ka-thumps progressed up the stairs and then down the hallway once more. This time I jumped up with greater dispatch and opened the door in an attempt to catch the mysterious person before he had a chance to vanish again. Once again there was nobody there. At this point I became quite curious about the vanishing intruder. I began to feel that someone was playing a joke on me. Rapidly and methodically, I searched the upstairs, the attic, and the downstairs of the old estate. I scanned out each window as I passed it to try to catch a glimpse of the villain sneakily departing the premises. There was no one anywhere, and no sign or sound to hint of anybody's passing presence.

It began to dawn on me that there was something odd about the ka-thumpings; nevertheless, I went back to work. Then it happened a third time. It was the same sound and sequence—the same impression of somebody walking deliberately, methodically, with heavy steps, up the stairs, then starting down the hallway. This third time, I waited a little longer to open my office door. First I made certain that the sound of the ka-thumping was progressing surely down the hallway, and then in the midst of a ka-thump I threw open the door so I could instantly see the entire upstairs hall. I saw nothing; there was no sign of anything or anybody, and nothing stirred except the summer morning breeze. The ka-thumping stopped the instant I opened my office door. With by-then-practiced speed, I searched and scanned everything. There was no way he could have escaped, but I saw not a human soul. I lingered a while, but nothing more happened.

In fact, nothing else mysterious ever happened to me again in the house, although I had an office there for several more years and was often there at odd hours. Others, too, have been in offices there for years since then, but I am aware of no reports of inexplicable ka-thumpings or other mysterious phenomena. The house is used by scientists, however, so it would not be surprising to find that such things had actually transpired and were not reported for reasons of scientific propriety and sobriety.

Nevertheless, my experience that summer morning was very real, and there is no doubt in my mind that some phenomenon did occur. Three times within a fifteen-minute period, something made the unmistakable noise of heavy and methodical treading that progressed up the stairway and then down the hall.

My experience was so vivid that when I was there afterward I was always prepared to see something or hear something more, but I never did. I never treated the house quite the same way after that. I always felt that there was possibly something going on there beyond my normal ability to understand. The house took on a different hue for me; it acquired a sort of presence, almost as though it had consciousness. I never had any sense of malevolence about either the experience or the house. The emotional impact of the experience stemmed from the unexpected nature of the rapid passage from naively wondering who was around the old house so early in the morning to a full-blown, previously unimaginable confrontation with the inexplicable. The suddenness of the experience, just as when an accident happens, left me dazed and changed the way I looked at the world.

There was a time when I believed in a strictly mechanical sort of reality—the normal world of the senses. Now, however, the notion that material reality—the palpable, touchable—is the only reality seems dull. After the eye-opening experience of that morning, I came to be able to see things in a different way, enabling me to have a number of experiences in my life that I otherwise would not have had. That morning left me believing that what we experience as the normal, material world is only a partial view of some larger reality.

The irony of the experience is that the incident took place on the grounds of a prestigious, world-renowned scientific institution. People there work to understand nature using the techniques of scientific methodology and rational objectivity. The work of the scientists in Woods Hole is scientific and rational, but what happened to me that summer morning was neither scientific nor rational.

HOLD YOUR HORSES

On the grounds of Mashpee's Maushop Stables, horses, rabbits, cats, dogs, and goats were more commonly seen than people. Similarly, reports of spectral animals on the property abounded. Robin and Jim Blakeman, former managers of Maushop Stables, said they became so used to constant animal sounds that it was hard for them to distinguish what might have been phantom hoof beats from the noises made by flesh-and-blood animals—except at night, when the horses were locked in their stalls.

Robin recalled hearing the sound of galloping horses behind her house on the Maushop property in the pre-dawn hours.

Her husband, Jim, will never forget one winter night, when he went up to one of the stable buildings to check on a sick horse, and encountered more than just noises. It was ten o'clock at night. Robin was in bed. Jim got dressed and went up there with a flashlight. It was cold out, so the doors at the back of the barn were closed. Jim used the flashlight in the long, dark, narrow hallway of the stable to illuminate the cement floor and cobwebbed, dingy white walls, instead of turning on the inside lights, which would have disturbed the horses. "I shined the light," he said, "and I looked up, and standing on the outside facing me was a horse that I thought was stalled in this barn, down at the end stall on the right.

"I said, 'Ah, Hotshot, you got loose.' I figured, 'When I'm finished, I'll go get him and put him away.' I went in the stall, and as I was checking on Ginger, I heard clip-clop, clip-clop, clip-clop. I came out and said, 'Oh, no, you don't.' I caught him on the shoulder, and I pushed. I ran my hand all the way down him, right to the tail. And he got by me. I said, 'Aw, no, I'm gonna have to get grain in a coffee can'—you shake it and they come running. So I checked all the stalls and everything, running around making sure everyone was okay."

When Jim reached the last stall, the one with Hotshot's name on it, he instinctively stepped toward it to retrieve the horse's halter. He was in for a shock. The door was bolted shut. He looked inside, and Hotshot was still there. "That's when the hair on the back of my neck stood up, and I did a very quick walk down to the house. I walked in, and I opened the bedroom door. Robin asked, 'Hey, how's Ginger? Are you okay? You look kind of pale.'"

Jim's hands were shaking as he told his wife the story. His hands were also covered with the black film one gets when one rubs a horse. The next day Jim checked with nearby stables and confirmed that there were no loose horses that night. A couple of days later, Robin and Jim were going through old photos when Jim saw a snapshot of a large horse that looked exactly like the horse he'd seen. Robin identified the horse as

Cinnamon, who had died many years before. She said, "You probably just met Cinnamon."

Apparently, Jim's experience was not the only appearance of the spirit pony. A former employee named Laurie was standing with a couple of teenage stable hands at the end of the barn one night, when they saw a red pony go into one of the paddocks. They went to close the gate to keep him in, but when they got to the paddock, there were no horses inside.

Many who lived and worked at the stables felt the grounds were home to several human spirits as well, including a former manager, who paced the floorboards of his upstairs office, and Gladys, a stout, white-haired woman wearing an apron who haunted a former stable and tack room that was converted into a house for her and her husband in the 1950s. Gladys had been known to sit in a bedroom chair on occasion and was said to clank objects together in the kitchen to let the current occupants know that the dishes hadn't been done.

The secluded spot ringed by hilly pine forest is the site of thousands of years of continuous human habitation. One of the last bastions of Mashpee's Wampanoag Indians, the grounds border a tract of Indian sacred land. Some residents and stable workers reported hearing phantom Indian drumming. Robin's young daughter Michelle claimed that she and her little brother were scared away from the woods one day by the drumbeats.

Robin has her own philosophy that allowed her to walk the grounds at night without being scared. "If you, in your heart, are looking for good, only good spirits are going to mess with you."

THEATRICS

Ask the longtime members of the Falmouth Theatre Guild what they enjoy about their troupe, and they'll gush about the camaraderie and sense of purpose leading up to a production. In the process of building the set and lighting, designing costumes, recruiting the cast, and, of course, rehearsing their roles, doctors, waiters, accountants, store clerks, and secretaries have built tight friendships that they might not have found elsewhere. When they routinely work deep into the night, many in the company feel a ghost, Faye, is watching over them.

Founded in 1957, the nonprofit theater group moved into the Highfield Theatre in 1960 with three performances of "Stalag 17" directed by William D. Steele. "We went through a lot," said Kitty Baker, who was president of the Guild in those early days. "The roof leaked. We would go upstairs and there would be mice running about and several buckets of water. We had snow coming down right through the roof in the middle of one show. It was adventuresome. We had a good time."

Despite the hardships, a number of individuals with theater in their blood stayed on. More than one would drag along their kids and include them in productions. A few have remained active with the troupe for several decades, but hardly a soul in the Guild questions that Faye has been around the longest.

Bordering an entrance to the nature trails leading into the Beebe Woods, the Highfield Theatre, Faye's stomping grounds, is a former barn with an old stone foundation, gray siding, casement windows, red doors, and a courtyard that is abuzz before and after the thrice-per-year productions. The house part of the theater is an addition with three hundred seats brought over in 1947 from the Tremont Street Theatre in Boston. Sight lines are challenging because the seats were installed one behind the other, but building acoustics are outstanding, and few would deny that the productions are entertaining and of very high caliber for community theater.

According to local legend, Faye was a member of the Beebe family, who lived in the renowned Highfield Hall, near the theater, from 1878 to 1932. She fell in love with a stable hand. When the family found out, they fired Faye's lover and she hanged herself in the tower house, a mansion outbuilding that the Guild uses for costume storage. Historical evidence to support this is as elusive as proof of the existence of ghosts. Still, most Guild members swear by the story and credit Faye for a number of curious things that happen in the Highfield Theatre. In the wintertime, the stage curtain is kept closed while the entourage is rehearsing or painting scenery. While people are busy at work, they often hear the seats falling open. But when they look through the curtain, the seats are still up. "One time, I was backstage alone preparing the set and it was like someone was beating on a drum," said Vicki Engstrom, who served in many different capacities in the theater from 1983 to 1991. "The seats were just going down. It spooked me to the point where I just got out of there."

Vicki was alone in the theater one afternoon in February, and there appeared to be no one next door at the Beebe Woods Facility for the Cape Cod Conservatory. No other cars were in the parking lot. Vicki was in the dressing room sewing costumes when she started hearing music. It sounded like it was in the background, like a pianist playing in a nightclub. She called out, "Hello, I'm up here!" Nobody responded. She went down the stairs, across the stage, and out the stage door entrance and found nobody. Returning to the dressing room, she heard the sound again. She opened the dressing room's exit door and looked out back and saw no one. It unnerved her enough that she decided to go home.

Some feel that Faye leaves with them. The spirited ghost has been known to accompany Guild members part of the way home. "She does that more if you've been here awhile," said Debbie Haynes. "You get the eerie feeling someone is in the car with you until you get down to the stone pillars at the end of the property."

Debbie has been with the Guild since 1979 and now sits on the board of directors. She remembered back to when she was just seventeen and was dropping off some sand for a set on what, she felt sure, was an empty stage. There was a drop hanging, and from behind the drop there was a tremendous bang, as if one of the lights had fallen. She went behind the drop and found nothing out of place. She says there is no rhyme or reason to Faye's appearances, although during *No Sex Please, We're British*, the lights in the house would always flicker in rehearsal during the opening scene.

"I've never really seen Faye, but I think she's there," said Gil Rapoza, who has been with the Guild for about forty years. "Sometimes during performances, the lights would go off and we'd know why. I get a little nervous being there by myself. I used to leave the door open and the light on."

"She doesn't bother me anymore," said Debbie. "She does frustrate me a little bit when she turns the lights back on in the prop loft late at night. You shut the lights off in the loft, and you go down into the theater and the lights are back on. When you're trying to get out of there and it's 12:30 at night, the last thing you want is her playing with the lights."

Faye has also been seen at Highfield Hall. College Light Opera Company (affectionately dubbed "CLOC" by locals) fills Highfield Theatre during the summer with their music theater and operettas, and the Oberlin Gilbert and Sullivan Players used to stay in the otherwise vacant Queen Anne mansion. According to Ursula Haslun, who runs CLOC with her husband, Robert, one day in 1967, the set designer was painting a portrait on the second-floor landing, for which there was only one staircase, when a woman wearing old-fashioned clothing came walking by. She said, "Hello, do you mind if I just look around? I used to live here." She went into one of the bedrooms. After a while the set designer wondered why she hadn't come out. He went into the bedroom, and no one was there.

The only other rumored appearances of Faye have been during Theatre Guild rehearsals. Guild members have been onstage with the doors locked and looked to the back of the auditorium and seen a white puff of smoke that resembles a form.

Robert Haslun, who also serves as secretary of the college at Oberlin, wondered if it's all just the artists' imagination running wild. "It's a very old building," he said. "There are all sorts of noises because it's filled with raccoons and critters."

Vicki Engstrom admitted there is an oral tradition of stories passed down from veteran Theatre Guild members to newer members. "Theater has a lot of drama in it," she added. "But I know raccoons aren't dropping the seats and playing music in the walls."

Vicki shared that when the Guild did Bram Stoker's *Dracula*, they were having a production meeting in the theater at dusk on a Sunday evening when everyone present heard the squeaks and flutters of bats leaving their roost in the cupola over the stage to go hunting in the evening. "The irony was that it had never, to our knowledge, happened before," said Vicki, "but it happened in a production meeting for *Dracula*, the ultimate classic vampire play. It was just something unique and so typical of the ghostly events that seemed to happen in every production. Perhaps they could be explained with logic, but it would be hard to convince the people who have experienced these happenings. I don't recall spending a whole lot of time sitting down talking about that stuff. It was always about what play we were doing and what places we were in at the time, getting the lights up, and making sure the heater was going."

"Faye just adds a little something extra," said Debbie. "She's our mascot."

ACKNOWLEDGMENTS

One of the most rewarding aspects of this project was getting to know people whom we otherwise may never have met. We started our research in the winter of 1994 by contacting historical societies and visiting libraries, town halls, fire stations, nursing homes, VFW Posts, artists' studios, and local diners. In almost every setting, we were fortunate to come across people willing to point us in the right direction. Many individuals said they saw a need for a more substantive book on haunted houses and spurred us on. Some went as far as to make phone calls on our behalf and even take us to the homes of friends who had stories. The kindness and enthusiasm of strangers was exactly the reassurance we needed to stay the course with our research. Sitting down to talk with our interviewees, often in their cozy antique homes, was delightful. The line between interview and familiar conversation would often blur, as people opened up about their experiences, feelings, beliefs, and lives in general.

We extend our heartfelt thanks to all of our interviewees

and their families for making us feel welcome in their homes during the hours spent talking and reviewing chapters. We were moved by the generosity, warmth, and trust they showed us.

We'd also like to express our gratitude to the following historical societies and a few individuals in particular, who greatly aided our research: Karen Adams of the Osterville Historical Society, Patricia Anderson of the Barnstable Historic Commission, Barbara Gill of the Sandwich Archives and Historical Center, and Priscilla Gregory of the Historical Society of Yarmouth. The efforts of Bonnie Snow of the Orleans Historical Society set our project in motion, and it would be a much lesser book without her kindness. Special thanks also to Bill Neilsen and Mary Ann Wyley of the Brewster Historical Society, Beverly Thatcher and several other committed volunteers at the Harwich Historical Society, and Helen Olsen and Bud Turner of the Wellfleet Historic Society. We also received help and leads from the historical societies of Barnstable, Centerville, Cotuit and Santuit, and Eastham.

Local libraries and archives proved an invaluable source of stories and reference materials, and we are indebted to the staffs of Chatham Library, Cotuit Library Association, Falmouth Public Library, Hyannis Public Library, Wilkens Library at Cape Cod Community College, Sturgis Library, Sandwich Town Archives, and the *Cape Cod Times* archives department.

Additional research help was given by Doris Alms, Kitty Baker, Roberta Bradner, Ed Brennan, Dan Buckley, Steve and Janet Chalmers, Betsy Cochrane of *The Register*, Freeman Crosby, Paul Cunningham, Arnold Dyer, Ruth Eddy, Brenda Figueredo, Paul Fortin, Debbie Gray, Dr. James Gould,

Matthew Gould, Doug and Sugar Manchester, Helen Mourton, Janet Nicholson, Robert Oldale, Susan Shephard, Jill Slaymaker, Dorothy Svenning, Jane Waggoner, Betty Walker, and Arlene and Richard Weckler.

The advice, encouragement, and support of the following persons were vital to the successful completion of this project: Sheila Bearse, Barbara Brydenpack, Richard Chandler, Fredda and Roger Chauvette, Admont Clark, Christine Connors, Linda Coombs, Jay Critchley, Danny Davis, Laurene DeMaire, Brian Dunne, Eric Edwards, Capt. Thomas A. Ferreira, Darlene Flood, George Gmelch, Dr. Paul Goldring, Andy Gordon, June Gordon, Al Guibord, Eleanor Henderson, Linda Hoffman, Mary Houk, Hiromi "Mikki" Lima, Lee Lockwood, Pia Mackenzie, Byrdine Melton, Don Metz, Henry Morlock, Sarfaraz Nawaz, Paul Noonan, Sam O'Hara, Tim O'Hara, Barbara O'Neill, Michael Parlante, Ramona Peters, Helen Picard, Ruth Ribner, Dawn Rickman at Wellfleet Town Hall, Sarah Rivers, Candyce Rusk, Ed and Shirley Sabin, Nancy Vivante, and James Wolff.

Additional thanks go to those who read parts or all of the manuscript: Rachel Alexander-Hill, Ron Bachman, Jerry Beck, Mickey Bradley, Dianne Burnham, Alexis Dolock, Dr. Charles Foster, Shirley Gennari, Betsy Gitelman, Julie Gordon, Paul Hodash, Pico Iyer, Jacqueline Joseph, Larry Kessenich, Uta Lausberg, Barbara McCullough, Brian McKeown, Holly Nadler, Martha O'Hara, Glenda Ritterhaus, Tony Supriano, and Lucy Whitmarsh.

We particularly want to single out Dan's writers group; his fellow members' support, praise, and constructive criticism inspired us toward higher standards.

We are indebted to Adam Gamble for his helpful suggestions on how to improve our manuscript. The Revolving Museum also contributed tremendously to our project by supporting Dan as writer-in-residence.

Special thanks go to Gerald Joseph for lending Dan his sofa, to the spirited conductors of the 11:59 P.M. South Attleboro commuter rail local for their consistent good humor as Dan rode home tired after long writing days in Boston, and to the crew at Ethier Way for affording Dan the opportunity to write and reminding him not to forget his book bag.

Scott Coughlin, Bayla Fine, Gloria Fitzsimmons, Ann Medeiros, John O'Hara, Stephanie Shea, Ken St. Don, and Jeffrey Wrobel saved our skin during countless computer crises.

We are deeply grateful to Alan Dewar and Steve Smith for giving us the chance to meet in the first place.

We pause to honor the memories of the late Lee Baldwin, J. Russell Chase, Frank James, Kathleen Pratt, Ruth Rickmers, Margaret Servideo, and Professor Brad Fisk, who advised Gary to write about the why as well as the what.

We appreciate the artistry and technical skill of several talented individuals. Wendell Minor added another beautifully rendered, soulful cover to his already remarkable body of work. Brian Barth's text design provided dignity and professional polish. Kate Bresnahan and Hannah Gaw consistently dazzled us with their copyediting wizardry.

We offer our sincere apologies to any person or group we may have overlooked.

Finally, we'd like to express our gratitude to the past inhabitants of Cape Cod for their enduring handiwork and for choosing to stay out of sight during the interviews. We wouldn't have a book without them.

ABOUT THE AUTHORS

Dan Gordon first experienced the magic of the Cape as a child vacationing two weeks each summer in Chatham. His admiration for the Cape's soulful homes inspired him to spend the last decade researching the Cape's ghost stories. He has covered global baseball for the *Providence Journal-Bulletin*, writing pieces that appeared in the Sunday magazine supplement and were used over Scripps-Howard Wire Service. His work also appears in *Elysian Fields Quarterly* and *Nine: A Journal of Baseball History and Culture*. *Scribner Encyclopedia of American Lives: Sports Figures* published his profile of Pedro Martinez. Gordon is currently working on a coming-of-age travel memoir, *Around the Horn: Voices of Baseball from Cuba to Japan*.

Gary Joseph, a lifelong Cape resident, has long been interested in accounts of ghost encounters. As a child, he enjoyed listening to adults tell these stories and observing the way people told them—their expressions, their mannerisms, and how they captivated an audience. He also writes about film, natural history, and the outdoors.